The Circle Game

RESEARCH TEAM

Senior Research Associate

DONNA GRIMALDI

Research Associates

STEVE ARRUDA

CYNTHIA KROUSKROUP

Research Assistants

CAROLE E. ASKER

JAMES BARNEY

BETTY DELANEY

ANTHONY DI PERRY

JUDITH FERTITTA

NANCY HACHEY

JOHN JOHNSON

NANCY LENOCI

MARY ROSELLA O'KEEFE

MARY QUINN

SUSAN ROTONDO

ANTHONY F. SANTIO

ANDREW WALKER

ELEANOR WALKER

The Circle Game

Services for the Poor in Massachusetts,
1966–1978

ANN WITHORN

The University of Massachusetts Press
Amherst, 1982

Copyright © 1982 by
The University of Massachusetts Press
All rights reserved
Printed in the United States of America
Library of Congress Cataloging in Publication Data
Withorn, Ann, 1947–
The circle game.
Includes index.
1. Social service—Massachusetts. 2. Massachusetts—
Social policy. 3. Poor—Services for—Massachusetts.
I. Title.
HV98.M39W57   362.5′56′09744   82–6926
ISBN 0–87023–376–9   AACR2

For
Betty and Mary Jo
The Yenching Collective

Acknowledgments

This study grows out of much collective effort. In January 1979, after the election of a new governor of Massachusetts, I decided to write a recent history of human services in Massachusetts. The goal was to provide a base from which to view the changes wrought by the new administration. A group of thirteen students at the College of Public and Community Service of the University of Massachusetts/Boston (all adults, with experience in human services) took up the initial research tasks and gathered great quantities of information. With leadership from Donna Grimaldi, they were also extremely important in suggesting ways to focus the history and make it more organized. A year later, in the spring of 1980, another group of CPCS students read a rough draft. With their help and the continuing support of Donna Grimaldi, I was able to write another more coherent draft. During the final stages of research, Steve Arruda and Cynthia Krouskroup provided invaluable assistance in seeking missing information and in sharpening the questions.

In short, this book could not have been written without the students at CPCS who did much of the research, and by the large numbers of them who read the drafts and responded with comments. In addition, over thirty students at the college allowed themselves to be interviewed. I was inspired by everyone and drew energy from their perseverance and ability to keep fighting.

As the scope of the project became clear, many others offered their assistance. Betty Mandell and Mary Jo Hetzel read all drafts and offered extensive comments, political criticisms, and editorial suggestions. Rochelle Lefkowitz did substantial editorial work on both drafts. Clark Taylor, Ilana Lescohier, and Nancy Aries offered helpful suggestions on the rather embarrassing first draft. Aileen Hart and John Romanyshyn read and assisted in providing focus to the second draft. Robert Morris provided inspiration and a sense of limits. Lennie Marcus shared his recent work on DSS. CPCS faculty and staff were generally helpful in allowing me to keep my sanity. Marilyn Metro provided both typing and critical services which were invaluable to all drafts. Ruth Anderson typed most of the final copy. Joanne Pearlman was tolerant every time I abandoned our mutual responsibilities to do "one last interview." My dean, Murray Frank, always gave me support and a sense that the study was important to the college. Leone Stein, at the University of Massachusetts Press, was encouraging and patient with her nervous fledgling author. And George Abbott White always forced me to respond to his fundamentally anarchistic critique of the bureaucracy in a way that kept this study more humane.

These are the people who helped me write this study. Then there are the dozens of others who shared the insights, reactions, and experiences that gave this study its life. I cannot name all of them here. However, I do want to acknowledge the special help offered by Robert Ott, Steven Minter, and Alexander Sharp, all former welfare commissioners who were exceptionally open and willing to explore hard questions.

The book owes its range and vitality to the contributions of many. Its shortcomings and misconceptions are entirely my own.

Ann Withorn

Boston, January 1982

Contents

Foreword

Human service programs, despite their diversity, if taken together constitute one of the major economic and social sectors of modern industrial societies. In the United States, about one-fifth of the gross national product may be accounted for by this sector, with its income transfers, funding of food, shelter, and clothing purchases, and its payrolls. In Massachusetts, such programs may account for half of all state public expenditures. It is remarkable that so large a part of modern society still lacks consistent or penetrating historical treatment. Can this be a sign of denial of human difficulty which blinds not only the common citizen but social scientists as well?

The Circle Game is a valuable addition to scant historical literature about the painful struggle of citizens, public officials, service workers, and the poor or troubled to come to human terms with each other's existence. The volume is in the noble, but limited, tradition of past efforts to maintain some record of the evolution of social programs. There have been a few landmark works about national trends, such as those by Chambers, Lubov, and Leiby, but not since the important University of Chicago Social Service Monograph series of the 1930s has there been a major attempt to document state and local level historical developments which constitute the foundation blocks for our human service systems. It is at this level that professionals and citizens require a historical memory.

The conclusions of this volume—that the preoccupations of the daily moment obscure the gains as well as the losses, as strong forces seek to shape and reshape welfare systems—enhance the few earlier studies. In 1938 David Schneider, writing about New York State, wrote of "the heartbreaking persistence of the same old blunders and half-baked experiments in economic crises repeated in spite of the plain evidence of past experience. . . . In spite of cycles and fluctuations, there has been a gradual progression" (*The History of Public Welfare in New York State, 1609–1866* [Chicago: University of Chicago Press, 1938]). And in 1939, Sophonisba Breckenridge wrote "It is a painful experience, setting out and then viewing the varied confusing and confused actions taken [in Illinois]. . . . It is believed that a study of this halting and complicated response to the need of persons, whether with or without fault on their own part, will reward those who look for a better day . . ." (*The Illinois Poor Law and Its Administration* [Chicago: University of Chicago Press, 1939]).

Studying or recording the evolution of social welfare programs calls for a special blend of empathy for the conditions under which troubled clients and overworked staffs live each day; for a realistic grasp of the complexity of bureaucratic organization and of the political/economic pressures which beset social policy making; and for a critical eye. To these talents, the author of *The Circle Game* brings as well a sense of irony, hope, and compassion.

Aside from the basic conclusions about the presence or absence of positive change, there are several lessons to be gleaned from this recent history, and each is worth an additional comment. From the historical perspective of social welfare, it is especially valuable to be reminded that underneath all the pulling and hauling of political factions there exists a basic struggle to define for poor people the importance of money (or its in-kind equivalent in Medicaid or food stamps) as a respectable service in its own right which should be provided in a humane society by means which maintain or restore the self-respect and dignity of its recipients. It is proper to consider the generic Department of Public Welfare as the sick patient of social history until this basic understanding is accepted. It is sobering, for social workers recall that in the 1930s a few pioneers, among them Grace Marcus, argued that the administration of public assistance was a function calling for high skill if the destructive possibilities of dependency are to be prevented. This view governed the early days of our then-new nationally based public assistance efforts. It is sad to learn how this lesson was lost in the 1960s and 1970s as public interest in these programs receded, as people became impatient with the persistence of economic need, and as they turned more and more (at least the political leadership did) to techniques of business management, changing the administration of relief into a depersonalizing, often degrading, clerical function in which few agency staff had time for the human beings they were to serve. In light of such forgetfulness, it is heartening to find the hope which remains, that a public assistance agency which is divested of many other more popular tasks (such as treating clients psychosocially) has a new opportunity to regain its own human function after a decade and a half of upheaval.

A second lesson from this period is that any effort to restructure large complex systems with minimal means and unclear goals is not only vastly time-consuming, but also produces confusions and unexpected, unwanted consequences. In Massachusetts, the piece-meal restructuring led to several years of confusion among agencies, to a drop in staff morale, to increased turn-over and disillusionment—in large part because the course of change and the desired or sought-after goals were unclear. Such confusion is in part a result of the compromises that had to be made about the nature of reorganization and about the tools which would be given for carrying it out. As a result, changes proceeded by fits and starts. Often, as in the case of Youth Services and Mental Health, new programs were initiated without much preparation for what their clientele would need under new regimes. Although it reasonably can be argued that such confusion is a fair price to pay if decisions are to be taken and changes made without dictatorial imposition from above, the fact remains that the cost is high both in dollars and in human value terms. Much of the ensuing freedom is the freedom of bureaucracies to maintain their separate prerogatives while slighting the human needs for which they are established.

A third lesson has to do with the tribulations of introducing proven and humanly valuable new directions, such as returning the mentally ill, the handicapped, and youthful offenders to service, care, or control in natural community settings rather than maintaining them in large, isolated, and personality-sapping institutions. Here, Massachusetts did pursue a persistent if uneven strategy of returning its services to mainstream communities where social pressures and supports of normal community life can reinforce the efforts of professional staffs to deal with very troubling human difficulties. In this instance, discharging people from institutions required that some transitional and in-the-community support systems be organized, offering personal services as well as income. The mentally ill, the retarded, the severely handicapped, the acting-out delinquent youth, the unemployed, and the poor will not just go away if their conditions are ignored or "discharged" or neglected. They are not thereby made more capable of adjusting to very complex living conditions. Their needs arise from the pressures which modern life fosters and from their personal limitations, either learned, innate, or imposed by adverse economic conditions. If they are to be given a place in a caring or human social order, appropriate help needs to be given, whether in institution or in community. Much of the history of the past decade has been a testimony of the struggle of a liberal state to realize such ends through imperfect social structures. To do better requires a fair income basis as much as professional personal services.

Given such difficulties and challenges, it is heartening to find a contemporary historian who has been part of history, who is able to see the beauties among the blemishes, the gains among the disappointments. The recent history has been one of trying to integrate and centralize essential social programs on a statewide basis, rather than relying—as in the sixteenth through nineteenth centuries—upon the local neighborhood and personal charity. The past two decades, at least, have been ones of trying out the utility of larger centralized organization along with new management techniques coupled with professional skills. By such means, the Massachusetts history has seen an equalizing of services across the state, a returning to community life of unnecessarily institutionalized citizens, tighter management of public funds, more personnel training, and the emergence of union protection for staffs. There has also been a proliferation in the variety and volume of services to deal with intractable problems, a result which may be trimmed by recent federal policies designed to roll back federal responsibility for social needs which are unlikely to disappear. It is important to note that such lifting of poor families from poverty as has occurred is due to income transfer programs such as public assistance, and not to the private sector of the economy. Between 1960 and 1977, the percentage of persons living below the poverty line fell from twenty to ten, which was due almost completely to public income transfer programs.

On the negative side of the balance sheet, most services are less personalized, staffs have been less secure in their work (with resulting costly rapid staff turn-over), costs have risen rather than been controlled (possibly because of the expense of centralized administration as much as from higher frontline staff salary or of increased service volume), and poverty—that underlying factor in the spread of most social problems—has not been abolished nor much diminished.

Poised between these positive and negative results are two other consequences: welfare costs have clearly been shifted from the local community to state and federal levels of government, making the burden less heavy on property owners, but also removing some of the problem from immediate view. And there has been a great increase in the tendency of government to give up its responsibility for administering social programs while turning over its tax revenues to voluntary, proprietary, or nonprofit agencies to administer mandated services. There is little evidence that such a structure is less costly, or more efficient, or that it meets human needs, in toto, any better than public administration; but the trend has distributed responsibility widely and may—over time— widen the constituency that can support the continuity of social programming.

At the end of a fascinating and frustrating fifteen years, it is timely to ask whether the state could proceed differently in the future. Here, the author introduces her own remedies and program for the future. It need only be noted that the tendency to blame most of these difficulties on the workings of the capitalist system, a common critique of many thoughtful persons, is only partly accurate. It is by now clear, as crossnational comparisons are made of programs in planned and in free or capitalist societies, that social programs involve control over deviant or dependent persons in all societies as much as they involve curing or caring for them. In both types of society, resources allocated for social purposes are limited. What may be more likely in planned societies (at least after the initial revolution which brought them into being), is the quality of central planning in which frequent, inconsistent organizational changes may be less common. As a result, social programs may have a greater stability regardless of the level of their adequacy. Such planned societies, with more centralized power, can also mandate resource distribution toward the bottom and down from the top to achieve a mean and flattened-out equality. The result is less diversity and more equality in condition, but not necessarily an average higher level of existence. Thus, stability and change are poised against each other, as are equality and equity.

In the end, regardless of the structure of an economy and a society, it now appears that the public treatment of serious social ills, and of economic as well as social deprivation, is still imperfect; the workable steps into the future are not clear even when objectives are crystal clear; and the planned structuring of mobile, fast-changing, complex industrial societies is still at a rather primitive level as far as providing for the human needs of the most vulnerable citizens are concerned. The social welfare giants and heroes of the past, who raised public consciousness about human needs, are still needed in the 1980s, and such reconstructions as this are essential equipment for them.

Robert Morris, DSW
Brandeis University

1 Introduction

I feel like one of the blind men trying to understand an elephant. I know day care, its rules and regulations, the people involved and the history of the past five years. But I don't know much about all of the other social services and I know even less about AFDC or Medicaid. And, when it comes to understanding how other agencies serve, or ought to serve, our families, I'm lost.

There are many people who feel like the Cambridge day care worker quoted above. She, like almost all the workers in Massachusetts's human service system, is a dedicated, hard-working woman who wants to provide the best services possible. She knows her own area well—its rules, legal constraints, history, and professional leadership. Yet she is often limited by her lack of a broader context from which to understand her experiences. Her plight is similar to that of the frustrated welfare mother whose teen-aged son is having difficulties:

I've learned how to live on welfare—how to fill out the forms and how to find the dentist who will take Medicaid patients. Even though it's hard, I've learned to survive. But now that my son is in trouble I have to learn about a whole new system—youth services, social services, the courts. Some of the rules are different, some are the same, but it's confusing and I don't know how it got this way or why it has to be so bad.

Both women may be hampered by their lack of knowledge about other services. If the day care worker wants to bring a consultant from the Department of Mental Health into her agency to help with troubled children she may encounter bureaucratic bottlenecks due to conflicting rules in different departments. If the boy is placed in a group home, his mother may find her welfare check reduced so that she cannot afford to visit him, as may be recommended when her son is placed.

Yet the state worker—who seems to be the bureaucrat causing

the problems for both women—may feel just as frustrated as they do. As one experienced supervisor explained:

We are stuck too. We are lucky if we have up-to-date manuals for the department's own regulations. We really don't know what's available through other departments. And even if we do have some idea, other agencies may feel they shouldn't directly help us, that it should go through channels. I just don't understand why it's so hard.

After all three encounter such roadblocks again and again they may begin to change. The day care worker may quit, or retreat into a less imaginative, more resigned, approach to her work. The supervisor may stop trying to work with other agencies or even become critical and defensive when younger workers—much less outsiders—suggest cooperation. And the woman on welfare? Her options are bleak and are likely, at least, to include anger and hostility toward such people as the supervisor and day care worker whom she encounters as they attempt to "help" her with her troubles.

This book is written to provide information to help sustain the day-care worker in her efforts to improve services in her community. It is written in the hope that if the supervisor knows more about why he is so isolated from other agencies he will be helped to resist frustration and be able to channel his anger in appropriate directions. And, finally, it is written out of a belief that if the welfare mother, the day-care worker, and the supervisor learn more, organize themselves and work together as peers they may find the strength to begin to change the rules and even the stakes of a system of human services that I call the Circle Game.

A Complex System with a Complicated History

It is not surprising that neither our day-care worker and administrator nor our client are fully aware of all aspects of the large and complex system maintained for helping the poor and needy in Massachusetts. The system contains a wide variety of programs that, since 1966, have taken up an increasingly large share of the state budget. Most state programs have been sustained, at least in part, by federal dollars and therefore have been governed by federal policies. But state funds are also allocated—under their own guidelines—to cover some programs fully, or to serve as a base for matching money from Washington. Local and private money is, in turn, invested, with its own stipulations, to supplement or match again state contributions. And the method and source of funding are different for each state agency and for different programs within each agency.

Yet, complicated and crucial as they are, funding patterns are but one source of the complexity that confuses workers, clients, and concerned citizens. For one thing, state agencies have very different histories and practices. Some date back to the turn of the century, while others are creations of the 1970s. In some older agencies, the quest for a professional work force and highly skilled patterns of treatment have remained constant themes. Newer agencies have often been more community oriented and employed a younger, more enthusiastic (and often lower paid) staff. Most agencies have been very hierarchical and centralized, but some have experimented with less predictable organizational forms. Directors of public and private agencies are usually aware of, and even competitive with, each other's programs. But, as we have seen, workers are often cut off from effective relationships with their counterparts in other agencies. In short, it is difficult to comprehend the whole system of interlocking agencies and programs established to serve the needs of Massachusetts residents—even if one is there every day.

The human service work force is varied also. At the top of most public and some prestigious private agencies is a group of well-paid, often highly educated, professionals from upper middle-class backgrounds. They know each other and, depending upon the governor, have varying levels of "political" connections. These people shuttle from Washington to Boston, from one upper-level agency to another. They view themselves as decision makers and policy makers and often hold national, as well as state, ambitions.[1]

Next, below the top leadership, are the upper- and middle-level administrative staff. This group has increased in numbers dramatically over the past twenty years. Their backgrounds are usually middle class.They are well educated and often define themselves more by their professional skills—lawyer, evaluation specialist, manager, planner, fiscal monitor—than by a concern for any special population. Some long-term service providers still move into these higher ranks, but, increasingly, they have been recruited directly from professional schools or from similar positions in other states.

Finally, there are thousands of service providers—from project directors and supervisors to service aides—who hold a wide variety of jobs. Some have little education and work in the homes of the elderly or handicapped to provide basic maintenance. Others work in day-care centers, halfway houses, and group homes, where they offer direct care to children, old people, the handicapped, and others needing direct assistance with daily living. Still others work within institutions and agencies, holding such jobs as counselors, youth workers, social workers, intake workers, or rehabilitation counselors. They help individuals meet their economic and social needs for financial assistance, recreation, transportation, community involvement, and counseling of many types. Some workers provide mandated services to those who may not want them, but have been legally judged to need care—such as juvenile services, some alcoholism and mental-health services, foster care, and so on. Veteran supervisors often oversee this activity, and give day-to-day direction to many programs. In many cases, local program directors have backgrounds in service delivery and serve as the link between higher authorities and direct-service staff. And there are the clerical workers who may seldom see clients but who spend their days processing the papers that allow services to be paid for and communication to flow among the various levels of service providers.

Often employees at different levels have little knowledge of each other and each other's work. Usually there is little information shared across agencies. So the human-service system can become—like the elephant in our day-care worker's example—a "management problem" to one person, a set of clinical case studies to another, and a list of state personnel line items to a third. The end result was aptly described by one highly placed administrator:

No one knows what you mean when you say "human services," you know. The public thinks either of welfare give-aways or retarded children. The legislators think of wasteful bureaucrats. Unions think of case loads and social workers think of diagnostic categories.

You can't have reasonable, informed discourse about something when everyone is talking about something different, but nobody knows it, or will admit to it.

Another level of diversity appears when we consider the widely different circumstances that bring people to receive these public services. Most, but not all, are poor—because there are financial eligibility standards applied to most programs—but they are all very different. Some are women who were once better off financially but whose husbands have left them with little support. Many are old. Many of the elderly are sick and have spent their savings. Great numbers are children. Still others suffer from physical or mental handicaps which contribute to their personal or family poverty. Some seek income only—the financial support to help them survive. Others want, or are judged to need, a wider range of services.

Just as the system of services looks different to different workers, so does it change perspectives for different client groups. Some know only their "own" agency; others have come to deal with many. Some spend much time and energy demanding services and pushing for more. Others struggle to avoid all contact and only participate in the system under great duress. As one veteran of many programs put it:

I've been there. I've been on welfare and SSI. I've dealt with Mass. Rehab. and with the Mental Health Center. I had to get day care for my kids and a nursing home for my mother. And I'll tell you, it's a trip. Some days you're so mad because they won't help you and others you're sick of them bothering you.

I want to get away but, then, I have to admit I couldn't have made it without them. I had no choice. I just wish I could have felt better about it.

This complex system which so disorients clients, frustrates workers, and confounds the public is not the brainchild of one governor, legislator, or upper-level administrator. There is no one to blame nor one grand design to praise. Underlying patterns exist, but the actual programs result from changes that have occurred piecemeal, resulting from varied pressures.

Yet, when we look at the contemporary history of this system we see changes that seem, in retrospect, quite dramatic. Since 1966, some agencies have changed their names and expanded their formats. New agencies have emerged. The entire organization of state government has been revamped. Reforms have been instituted to centralize state agencies; others have been designed to decentralize the same programs. New reforms have begun, been forgotten, been taken up again by new commissioners, and then, later, reshaped by still newer administrations. At the same time, old problems have perpetually re-emerged, such as the existence of child abuse and institutional abuse of residents, the problem of welfare "error rates," and the need for better training. Human service workers have consistently protested speed-ups and poor working conditions. Client advocacy groups have fought for different programs and opposed cutbacks, dispersed, only to regroup and fight again.

It appears, then, that the historical lessons also depend on one's place in the system. Some see that a great deal has changed in Massachusetts human services over the past few years. Others find that far less has altered. Even those who recognize changes offer different explanations of their meaning. Some see improved programs; others see a deteriorating environment for workers and the consumers of the system.

An intriguing pattern emerges. The further away people are from service delivery, the more likely they are to see progress. The closer people are to the actual service—either as consumers or providers—the more likely they are to find little change or a decline in quality. One state hospital worker's opinions are representative:

It's still the same old bull—no matter what new name they give it, people still show up here crazy as hell and we still don't have the supports, or know how to help them. We get a little more training, the wards look a little better and maybe patients stay here for a little less time, but our pay is still chickenfeed, our supervision is no use, and our ability to really do anything to help people is still nowhere.

Yet an upper-level mental health official argued, instead, that:

There can be no doubt that services have improved. The hospital populations are down. People are receiving, not ideal, but *better* care in the hospitals and in the community. Now we have hope for people who work in the system as well as for patients—hope that staff can learn more skills and that patients can live a more normal, less institutionalized life. Whatever the current difficulties, surely we can't deny this is progress.

An initial task for workers, clients, and citizens who want to alter the system is to decide what they think of developments that have already occurred. A review of the contradictory history of recent changes seems, therefore, to be essential before would-be reformers can conceive of new visions. This book is written with a hope that a more complex view of change can be achieved than just a narrow pessimistic dismissal or a privileged assertion of progress. Our title metaphor, to be discussed in the next chapters, arose out of just such an effort. A Circle Game can imply that things never change, that everything is actually the same. But circles can roll, too, and there may be some real sense of movement, even as patterns recur. The task of this book will be to examine which things change, and why; which have stayed the same and if there is something we can learn from the analysis that could help us alter the pattern.

The Need to Remember

Since 1970, I, too, have been involved in lesser and greater ways with the Massachusetts human services system. Then I was a young activist who did minimal support activity—dittoing, leaflet distribution—for a Cambridge welfare-rights organization. Later, I worked with teenagers, with Head Start parents, and with local service providers. I attended Welfare Coalition meetings and observed some of the professional leaders in their attempts to inform and influence the system. During the mid-seventies I used Brandeis University as a base from which to learn about and assist efforts to redesign social services in Massachusetts and elsewhere. I studied training needs and programs for social service workers, as well as radical and innovative programs for providing services. Through it all, I was often humbled and frustrated by my sense of how much there was to learn about even one state's system of services—and how hard it was to discover the roots of contemporary problems.

For one year (1977–78) I was intimately involved in an effort to design and deliver a large-scale training program to social service workers. During this year I met and observed more closely the interactions of state bureaucrats close to the top. The picture was puzzling and depressing. I worked with many dedicated people who wanted to improve service delivery by offering more training to state workers. Yet they, and I, were thwarted by an incredible mesh of conflicting mandates, interests, and goals. After this experience I vowed that, before I tried to act directly again within the bureaucracy, I would apply my hard-earned research and historian's skills to an attempt to understand how the Massachusetts human service system worked and why it seemed so difficult to accomplish anything.

Since the summer of 1978 I have worked with an ever-changing, but consistently impressive, group of adult students at the College of Public and Community Service, most of whom work in, or are clients of, the programs that have just been described. With their help, assistance, and insight for guidance I have engaged in a continued quest to examine and understand the dynamics of change within Massachusetts's complex web of service programs.

Historical analysis emerged as an effective way to accomplish this. As I talked with students and with colleagues I found that we all shared a frustration with our scattershot knowledge about the development of the programs within which we worked. So, spurred by the election of a new governor, I began the project that led to this book. In Appendix A I describe the method of inquiry; here what seems important is to note the reinforcement that came from all directions for a historical study. One woman articulated what many others expressed, in a note she wrote asking to participate in the project:

I don't know enough to fight. Even when I find out about all the programs around now, I don't know how they got that way. I'm lost when some-one says, "we've *always* done it this way," or "we tried that once and it was a disaster." So I want to find out more.

Yet as we began our inquiry we discovered a curious paradox. Most people expressed a need for history, for a shared memory of major events and developments. Yet, despite such widespread sen-timents, we found that most Massachusetts human service bureau-crats have been curiously lax in their record keeping. Over and over we found ourselves having to dig for data that we had thought would be simple to find. The amount of paperwork generated by agencies seemed to defy organization, so, ordinarily, no one tried to gather it together. Even when we asked the Executive Office of Human Services about its own staff and budgetary growth dur-ing its brief life, the answer was not easily available. Often we would be referred to an old veteran who was "a packrat and kept copies of everything," instead of to a formal office where the in-stitutional record was kept. Many tried to explain the problem to us: "Well, you see, we have a lot of turnover here and people take their files with them when they leave...," or "No one person is responsible for that. It's spread out in about three offices, so it's not clear who would be responsible for keeping the information in a permanent file."

Librarians at the State House library would refer us directly to the agency, because they only keep general-interest material. The agencies would tell us to try the State House library. We were con-tinually frustrated by the lack of a sense of history among agency personnel, among workers, and among clients. We began to won-der if we were wrong, if perhaps participants did not feel a need for their history. Finally, two different informants, from very different places in the system, were able to help us redefine the quest and also help us be more sympathetic to the lack of data. One was an upper-level welfare official who said:

Sure, we should keep a better sense of the history, but don't you see how hard that is? It's not just hard because the information is scattered and the agencies are structured so that no one place is a critical repository. No, it's hard because we all have to get up every day and go back to our jobs and try to make things a little bit better. If we were too aware of how much we were doing had been tried before, and failed, we'd be paralyzed, or cynical. That's why the old guy who remembers everything is back in a corner office with nothing to do. People are afraid of him and his "war stories." And often he is, indeed, unable to act because of all he knows.

Our other respondent was a former mental patient who was describing her experiences in various state hospitals to us: "It's like labor pains. If you remember them you can't even have another baby or help someone else have a baby. I think it's good you're going to tell the story but remember to make it *mean* something, otherwise it's just a bunch of sad things that are no use remembering."

Such comments made me—and our senior researcher, Donna Grimaldi—see how sensitive the need for remembering can become. The existing reality is overwhelming in itself; if we only add a recounting of past failures, people may become even more depressed by reminders of things left undone. Thus the goal expanded, our contemporary history became also a commentary, an attempt to move beyond the historical record and to suggest its implications for the future.

Current Contradictions

The need for analysis and commentary on the history is further heightened by developments in the years after 1978, when our account stops. Since then, such dramatic events have occurred that one sympathetic reader was compelled to comment:

What you really have is a "period piece" about a time which was unique and is gone forever. What's happening now has nothing to do with the dynamics of the Circle Game. It's a new game with new players, new rules, and new assumptions. The best you can do is to capture the past, describe it, and explain why it will never come again.

As a student of history, I am naturally skeptical of any argument that asserts that we have entered a new age, free from the constraints of the past, but in this case I can understand the skepticism. Since 1978, a new governor has brought different personalities to state government and has attempted to revive earlier approaches. This, alone, would not have been enough to radically change a system so complex and so influenced by forces outside itself. But the passage of Proposition 2½ and the election of Ronald Reagan provide a "double whammy" which works in harmony with the governor's aspirations of creating wrenching new pressures within the system.

Proposition 2½ represents a taxpayers' revolt against many of the problems with Massachusetts government that we, too, find when we examine the human services system.[2] However, the solution it embodies (especially in the short run and without ameliorating tax reform) is inadequate. It brings new actors into the arena, actors whose concerns are budgetary, not programmatic. So the wrong questions are raised, with little hope for better answers.

Under the new pressures created by Proposition 2½, it is difficult to launch a discussion regarding the substance of human service programs. Instead, the only relevant "fact" becomes the need for the state to cut social programs because cities and towns need relief from voter inflicted reform. In chapter 8 we will return to the problems inspired by 2½, in light of a full analysis of the system. We need only acknowledge that this shift in funding priorities since our study exaggerates the problems highlighted here and gives credence to the call for "new solutions."

The Reagan administration, as spearhead for a national New Right approach to government in general and social welfare in particular, proposes even more fundamental upheavals for the existing structure.[3] Again, we will return to these concerns later, but as introduction we should acknowledge the extent of the Reagan assault on the current national system of services, of which Massachusetts is but one piece. The relationship between federal and state programs, the list of mandated proposals and procedures, even the basic goals of the system, are being questioned by a set of well-informed administrators who know all the weaknesses and contradictions of the existing order. The extent of their success is yet to be determined. But the very boldness of their approach, and the openness of their disrespect for existing patterns, suggest that the upcoming struggle—if not the results—will be different from any we have undergone for fifty years.

However, it is the very seriousness of the challenge to the existing order that suggests that we cannot fail to seek lessons from the past.

First, we can recognize that it is not only Massachusetts that must change. Rather, the Circle Game is played, with local variations, in all other states. National studies indicate similar patterns of expenditures and comparable efforts to restructure and reorganize.[4] Our need to understand the specifics of our situation should not lead us to think we are an extreme case. At national conferences, indeed, human service officials usually sponsor at least one workshop or panel where debate erupts over which state is the most outrageous, the least amenable to reform. So Reagan's radicals must confront the vast sluggishness of entrenched systems which have been accruing set routines for decades, despite the surface turmoil.

It may be too early to tell, but many predict that conservative reformers will have the same difficulty making changes that their more progressive predecessors did.[5] So there remains a reason to understand, at least, what we might call the dynamics of inertia.

Second, on a more optimistic note, another reason for finding relevance in our past is to take advantage of the current turmoil. This book is written by and for people who want change every bit as much as the New Right does. The overriding premise, and conclusion, of this study is that something—not everything—is wrong. People in need do not get the services they require, offered in a manner that respects them. Workers are not able to fulfill the social impulses that attracted them to service work. Administrators are unable to manage and coordinate activities so as to create a more reasonable and effective system. Neither the judges nor the legislators really want the roles they have assumed. In short, the Commonwealth has far to go before it creates a caring society for all its members.

Times like these may allow us to be more open about the lessons from our past and to identify proposals for change that can be debated in opposition to suggestions from the Right. We cannot do this if we are ignorant about what does exist and where it came from. And, if we are not ignorant, we certainly cannot defend all that has gone before.

Limits and Uses of the Study

This study was not intended to produce a narrative full of surprises or exposés for insiders and the critical public. Nor was it to introduce a sophisticated statistical analysis of complex data for the use of academic policy analysts. Instead, it was meant to organize generally available information in a way that could be useful to concerned workers, administrators, clients, and human service activists. The chronology and general patterns are discussed and analyzed for the sake of understanding program developments and their current implications. Interview excerpts are used to highlight the human impact and dimensions of the changes, not to offer factual interpretations. In Appendix A the method is more fully described and the types of interviewees discussed.

The goal was to highlight and examine changes and continuities for human services in Massachusetts. We hoped to help people put their personal experiences into a broader context and to gain the energy to work for change. We tried to tell the story "straight," but also to draw upon our understanding of current tensions as a basis for our historical questions. Like any history, this review is influenced by our current sense of the issues facing service workers and clients today, although a serious attempt has been made to present the information so that others with different perspectives could make use of it. Finally, our hope is that many different administrators, workers, and clients will find confirmation of their experiences in these pages, as well as suggestions for how to interpret—and use—the past as a base for achieving change.

The bulk of the book is, then, a general case study of a particular system in a particular time. Chapter 2 presents the assumptions of the study as well as introduces the metaphor of the Circle Game and its rules. In addition, the chapter begins to explain the nature of the current system and the questions it raises about the past. Chapters 3 through 6 examine the historical developments and patterns in some detail. The final chapters summarize the best ways to understand the operations of the system as it was and suggest how we might face the future in light of the recent past. Always the stress has been on creating a general picture, not a highly specific, specialized analysis, out of a belief that, in many ways, our own specializations as administrators, workers, clients, and concerned citizens have kept us from seeing and understanding the overall impact of the Circle Game.

2   The Circle Game

Striking paradoxes are found in Massachusetts. It is a generous state. It is also a penurious and withholding one. It is a place where some needy people are treated with great kindness and understanding, and where others are treated with unconcern and coldness. [*Meeting the Problems of People in Massachusetts*, National Study Service, 1965]

Perhaps the most exciting aspect of doing this survey was the response we received when we asked people to remember back to thirteen or fourteen years ago. Most would start by insisting that they couldn't remember much. Then, at first slowly, and later more easily, the rush of remembering would begin. People were surprised at how much they could recall, how similar the issues then were to those of today, and yet how different the world seemed earlier.

We too were fascinated by precisely this overlap of change and apparent continuity. Some days we would be overwhelmed by how different everything was in 1966—days of civil-rights movements, the beginning of a War on Poverty and a war in Vietnam. And at other times, we would listen to the stories and think how similar they were to those of the present: the worries over costs, care for abused children and troubled youth, and uncertainty over how to administer complex programs. Indeed, we emerged from our research newly humble regarding the difficulty of changing bureaucracies and increasingly respectful of the women and men within the system (both workers and clients, administrators and citizen advocates) who try every day to bring about change while protecting and preserving the hard-learned lessons that have been formed over the years.

The Meaning of a Metaphor

The metaphor of the Circle Game emerged as we worked, as we heard comments like these:

Once we were very decentralized, then they reorganized us and set up a central structure. Just as we began to get used to that now they tell us we should decentralize again in order to provide better service. It gets pretty confusing. [Welfare worker, in system since 1963]

We started to offer runaway kids a place to be fairly comfortable and begin to get themselves together. Then we got a contract from the state to do this because we were good at it. Next they start pushing us to take more kids, because we're so good, but the kids they send us are not the kids we had been serving. So we now have more than we can handle and our staff turnover is high because the jobs are more impossible. And now the state is on our back because of the turnover and because we're not as good as we were. But they were the ones who pushed us to expand to take tougher kids. [Youth program worker]

I'm going back to school so I can get off welfare. I also need work experience in the health field so I can get the job I want. I'm eligible for work study which would allow me to get work experience in my neighborhood clinic. But the Welfare Department wants to deduct the money I make—which I am allowed to earn because of financial need—from my welfare budget. So I just can't afford to take the work study and get the experience I need. But if I can't find a job when I graduate, a WIN worker will make me take a waitressing job. It's all hopeless.[1] [Student welfare recipient]

The Feds have these fads. Suddenly they want everybody to have program goals all spelled out, or some new form of information reporting. They push and hint and pressure so we put our cumbersome process in gear and, after a year, we accomplish what they demand. But by then the fad is over, or the federal officer who was so enthusiastic has moved on and nobody cares. So the next time they come in with some new idea it's hard to get excited. [Upper-level welfare administrator]

Such sentiments were common. After we named our project and shared the name with interviewees, they usually knew immediately what we meant, often supporting us with yet another painful story:

It's a circle game, all right. Patients are mad at workers because of the rules here [a state hospital]. We feel we have to enforce the administrative rules or we lose our jobs. Then some advocacy group meets with the administrator and he backs down on his own rule and tells the people it's all really the staff's fault for being too rigid. But you can bet that if we tried to change the rule on our own we would have been out the door. You're right, it's a circle and you can't win for losing. [State hospital nurse]

The Circle Game means many things. It suggests that—despite all the activity—workers, administrators, and clients see little change for the better. Sometimes it implies that the rules always change back to what they were; other times, that one goal cancels out another. Or, a further variation is that you "run around in circles" producing work that matters little in the end. There are circles within circles—rules and traditions that isolate one set of workers from another, clients from workers, and administrators from daily reality. There are false promises and no-win loops. Finally, it often feels as if there is no way out.

Students of bureaucracy might argue that this is the normal type of behavior in complex organizational systems.[2] Maybe so. Certainly a complex set of factors creates the pattern: formal rules, informal practices, outdated traditions, habits of mind, punitive sanctions for nonconformity, class and cultural social relations, as well as a lack of alternative models.

Yet, perhaps awareness of the Circle Game can help workers, clients, and administrators find possibilities for change—the tangents, if you will, that may steer the circle in another direction or alter its shape. In our interviews we met people who gave support to this hope. One was a mental health worker with twenty years of community experience:

I've learned that the world doesn't stop if you say "no." Now when they want me to do the impossible I say "no, it's impossible, we have to do some other thing instead"—I always have an option ready. At first people were shocked but I've found that I usually win because they know I won't give in and that my suggestions usually work because I know the community.

Another was a mid-level administrator:

I wait. I keep up with what I think is important and when a new mandate comes out that will upset my program I just wait. I don't fight right away but I don't stop doing what I know works. I try to think about what, if anything, of the new demand I can incorporate. Then after a few weeks I tell them how I plan to implement their new scheme. I *tell* them without a hint that it might be a problem for them. I win without a fight almost all of the time because they need me and because I'm not generally fighting them, and because sometimes they did not even understand the point of their new command. It's still a game but I feel like it's possible to win and that keeps me going.

Others found some ability to resist the Circle in group solidarity with co-workers through the union:

We staff got together and said that something had to be done about the over-crowding which was making it impossible to work. We threatened to go to the press. Somehow some clients were transferred and some new space was "found." [Halfway house worker]

And, finally, some recipients found power in knowledge and in each other:

I was a "Child in Need of Services." I found out that I could become one because I couldn't live with my family; my mother was a little Hitler. I met some other kids and they told me which programs to ask for and what I was entitled to. It wasn't easy, but we stuck together and I got food, an education, and a way to survive.

As we suggested earlier, understanding that the system operates as a Circle Game does not demand a response of total pessimism. Workers, administrators, and clients have exerted power within the system and have, at times, achieved some small, and large, goals. But those who did so always had at least an unacknowledged awareness of the existence of the game and its rules. They made changes exactly because they understood the system but retained an ability either to break the rules or, more often, to use them against the game itself.

The Rules of the Game

In any game the rules are designed to allow players to lose as well as to win. Winning depends, first, on understanding one's own assumptions and how they are in conflict or harmony with the rules that operate the game. An interim strategy may be to identify those rules that are acceptable and, then, to use them to take advantage of all positive aspects of the game and to work against the more destructive rules. Finally, however, a new game may have to be designed, with new rules and perhaps even a new definition of winning.[3]

We start here with our assumptions about how the Circle Game works and the sources of confusion that affect its day-to-day operations. In the concluding chapter we will return to speculation about how we might make immediate and more long-term changes.

First, we assume that, in the system of human services that has evolved since 1935, everyone in need has basic rights to receive decent care from the state. This assumption is embedded in the Social Security Act of 1935, whereby the federal government guaranteed social insurance to the old and disabled, as well as some form of public assistance (albeit meager) to families with dependent children, the indigent elderly and disabled. Admittedly, our reading of the implications of the act is a broad one, not shared by everyone. We range even further from the norm when we argue that the obligation of government is constantly to improve the minimal level of care—meaning income maintenance and other support services necessary for survival—which must be provided by right.[4]

While we push the assumption to its limits, even Ronald Reagan and some on the Right claim to accept it, in principle. They just disagree over what is "true need" and what "care" must be provided to meet it. In this they join in the long line of debates that have occurred since the 1930s—debates about how much financial assistance and what types of services people are entitled to, as well as at what point of need they should become eligible for assistance and services.[5]

Much of the tension that is embedded in the Circle Game arises from different positions regarding these questions. There is disagreement within the general public. Within the bureaucracy, different individuals and groups of employees will take different positions, although seldom in open debate. Client groups and activists usually insist upon pushing for their own rights but have sometimes failed to assume the same position in regard to other claimants.

As important as such disputes over the appropriate level of entitlements are, however, an even more fundamental tension arises from our first assumption. Logically, it implies that there is a public obligation to provide income and services, by right. The state is not being "charitable" or benevolent in offering services. Rather, it is fulfilling one responsibility for which government is established —to use collective resources when individuals in the society cannot maintain themselves independently.

Following from this, we argue that it is as much a responsibility of the state to provide services as it is for it to provide roads, sewers, and other public utilities.[6] We, therefore, are naturally also entitled to criticize inadequate public performance in this area, as in any other. Recipients do not need to be grateful for services any more than they should be grateful for receiving mail. Workers and administrators are doing no one a "favor," they are performing basic obligations of the society.

Obviously, despite the Social Security Act and a host of further legislation, many people have not accepted this assumption. Some see any government intervention as intrinsically harmful, even if necessary. At best, many seem to feel that most recipients receive services out of benevolence and that only a far smaller core—the truly needy, the worthy poor—actually deserve services.[7] For all such people—many of whom work in the system and some of whom are even clients—many public services are optional activities adopted by a generous government, not really rights. And the obvious corollary, in times of economic crisis, is that many programs become "fiscal frills" that can no longer be afforded.

Our purpose here is not to engage in the full debate about the responsibility of the state and the rights of citizens. However, it is important that we recognize that these open and unstated disagreements regarding rights to services, and the responsibility of government to provide them, have concrete manifestations in the work place. One food-stamp worker spoke unwittingly of their effects at her job:

There are two different kinds of people at my office. Some of us think that people without money have a right to food stamps and that our job is to help them get as much as they are eligible for. Some other people seem to think that people should be grateful for whatever they get and that our job is to make sure we don't give anybody any more than they absolutely need. It's funny, but it makes a big difference how you look at it, even though none of us are trying to break the rules.

Given the special importance of money in our society as something which must always be *earned,* the tensions are most obvious around cash-payment programs. But similar disagreements surface in service areas also. Even workers who supported client concerns would suggest that clients should be "more grateful" or argue that they can't expect too much because services are "free," after all. Some recipients, too, would criticize others for "taking advantage" of all the benefits allowed them. The issue emerges full blown into the public-policy arena, for instance, when governors try to introduce "workfare" proposals so that welfare recipients can go to work to "earn" their welfare checks.

Here, we are suggesting that the Circle Game is often confusing because of such fundamental disagreements. And we argue that one way to criticize the system is to analyze which of its policies and programs actually help to create and further the principle of public responsibility and which ones ultimately undermine it.

Our second assumption is that disagreements over the causes of poverty and the need for services create fundamental contradictions within the human-service system. We argue that the roots of poverty and other social problems—like mental illness, delinquency, child abuse—are complex and are embedded in the country's economic and social structure. The needs for services result from far deeper causes than individual weakness or past failures of social programs.[8] Following this logic we conclude that we can only begin to truly eradicate poverty and other social difficulties after fundamental changes take place in the political economy and in prevailing attitudes toward nonwhites, women, the family, and working-class culture.

Obviously, there is wide political and social disagreement in this society with the broader implications of such a position. And, on the less self-consciously political level, there is a dominant cultural practice in this country of "blaming the victim"—to quote William Ryan's central work—and to blame the individual for his or her own situation.[9]

But on the level of bureaucratic and professional practice there is more stated agreement than we might expect. The notion of "social casework," in theory, implants into the heart of social work practice the notion that many individual problems result from social factors. For example, in 1980 the journal *Public Welfare*, published by the American Public Welfare Association, acknowledged that there were complex factors involved in poverty and other social problems—although they placed less emphasis than we on the economic factors.[10]

In spite of such seeming agreement with our approach, many professionals and agency leaders tend—perhaps in response to their sense of the broader public ideology—to argue that their programs can "cure" individuals who come to them. They imply that, if only funds were available, they could cure *all* such individuals. Instead, we would argue that the implication of our perspective is that social programs cannot cure the overall problems that they address. Human services can help people cope, and even help some individuals in some circumstances to overcome personal difficulties, but the broader social disorders that create mental illness, alcoholism, retardation, and juvenile delinquency are inherently beyond the scope of human service programs to solve.

In practice, disagreements over this issue cause great confusion in service agencies. A rise in the number of poor people is blamed on the inadequacy of welfare programs. Increases in reported child abuse lead to accusations against service programs and/or individual social workers. If clients do not "recover" from whatever ailed them it becomes their own fault for resisting treatment, or the fault of the worker's lack of training. Impossible standards are created for administrators, workers, and clients—standards that ultimately suggest that the existence of a demand for the service is itself evidence for "failure" of the service agency. One union official expressed the implications of the dilemma with poignancy:

We, too, want programs which will be more effective at dealing with child abuse, as the new agency promises to do. But we are worried about going blithely along with their promises—that if they only get enough money and have well trained enough workers they can end child abuse. Workers know we can't stop all child abuse, no matter what we do. If that's to be the goal of the new agency we know we will lose, and get blamed, eventually.

Once we tried to suggest our approach to an upper-level administrator:

You want us to say that no matter what we do we'll *always* have to spend money on these problems? No one will buy it. It's unacceptable politically.

We have to argue, at least, that we're "working toward" an end to child abuse, cerebral palsy, poverty, whatever. Otherwise, it looks like we are just accepting that there is nothing we can do.

And yet, if, after years of such false promises, the public begins to think there is "nothing we can do" and votes to cut public expenditures or to elect presidents who will, has so much been gained?

A third assumption relates to the second one. We *can* state that most social problems addressed by human service agencies are insoluble short of basic social change, without accepting that there is nothing we can do. Therefore, we still assume that human service agencies can help individuals to cope better with their difficulties and that some approaches can be determined to be better at this task than others. This is a critical companion to our second assumption because without it we could abandon the needy to their "fate."

Here disagreements are less widespread within the system. There are sometimes pressures from the outside society because it is difficult for workers and administrators to "prove" that what they are doing is worthwhile, especially if success is defined as "curing" problems. Oftentimes, the ready evidence of poor past practices and ill-delivered services is used (by the Left as well as the Right, unfortunately) to discredit all service efforts. Faced with such criticisms and realities, workers and clients can become discouraged and demoralized.[11]

Yet, it is a basic argument of this study that services *can* respond to human need and help people cope with their problems. If we argue that the public sector has a responsibility to try to do this, we cannot rig the game by secretly thinking that nothing can be done. Even if they cannot cure the roots of much human pain, on a day-to-day basis clients, workers, and administrators need to have a sense that they can do some things to alleviate suffering.

This implies another expectation that motivates this study: that human service programs can be improved. If welfare departments cannot end poverty in a capitalist economy, perhaps they can end the hunger, desperation, disrespect, and medical need that accompany poverty. If social services cannot end all wife beating in a violent, male-dominated society, perhaps they can end women's need to search for safe refuges when they are battered.

In other words, we have to play the Circle Game until we change it or find another way to meet the needs it addresses—however poorly. Clients in need know this: "Bad as it is, we can't do without welfare until they find another way to keep my family and me alive," said many recipients. Many workers stay because they know this, as one long-term mental health worker explains: "They won't get rid of me. No matter how bad they make it. If I weren't here, it would be worse for folks from my community and I'm going to stay. Somebody has to be there and it might as well be me." It is more likely to be the outsiders, knowing less of the pain and the need, who see all the flaws and want to throw it all away. Others stay on, fight, get discouraged, and try in little ways to make things better.

Our final assumption builds upon all the rest. It is that the failure to acknowledge that all human service goals cannot be met under this social system is the root cause of the problems with the Circle Game. This economy and this political and social structure have never accepted the level of monetary and social commitment that is required to address the underlying social problems that create needs for services. If politicians, the public, and social welfare officials would accept this they might be able to design a set of less contradictory services. Without our massive societal denial regarding the enormity of social needs we might be able to avoid the current, perpetual situation where no one can win.

Here, another metaphor may express it best, an image where the practice of human service is seen as that of a woman given some, but not enough, tiles to cover her floor. She ably covers one corner, but when she looks around and sees the parts of her floor left uncovered she quickly dismantles what she has done in order to cover the bare spot, only to look once more and see that most of the floor is still uncovered. As we can see, she is never able to cover the floor without more tiles, so the options left to her are difficult ones. She can scatter the tiles about the floor so that no one area is really covered but all areas have some tiles and then claim that the floor *is* covered; or she can cover those parts of the floor for which she has the tiles and announce that the bare spots don't need cover anyway (or even that those bare spots don't *deserve* cover); or she can create a few beautiful, flashy designs in the spots she is able to cover and hope that no one will notice the bare areas; or she can try a quick-change routine, spreading tiles in the area where people are looking, then quickly moving them to another corner as people start to look over there, abandoning the first spot where no one looks any more. We assume here that none of these options is adequate and that all create a process (dare we call it a cover up?) that leads to the Circle Game.

Yet there may be another option. Our floor coverer could admit out loud that she doesn't have enough tiles and explain how everyone will benefit from an adequately covered floor. She can do the best job possible in covering those areas of her floor where the traffic is greatest. Then, based on her success in covering the critical parts of her floor and on her convincing arguments about how much all could use a fully tiled floor, she may work with others both to create and to demand more tiles, even if it means taking some from the patio by the swimming pool of the mansion up the street.

Where We Have Come

The specific ways in which these assumptions have been played out in Massachusetts will be the subject of the rest of this book. But before we can effectively understand the past we need to formulate our questions out of the present reality. Therefore, we will briefly look at the current aspects of the human service system that suggest how we might evaluate the historical developments.

Who uses services, and why?

The 1980 census figures suggest that there are approximately 595,600 poor people in Massachusetts, out of a population of 5,737,000. There are over 726,531 individuals over sixty-five years of age, many of whom may find themselves in need of public services in the next decade.

In December 1980, there were about 6,400 people in state mental hospitals and schools for the retarded. Approximately 7,000 children were in foster care or some form of institutional placement. Of the poor, 330,000 were on welfare (AFDC), 66 percent being children and most of the rest being their mothers, with a few unemployed fathers included. Other agencies reported serving—either directly or through private programs that have contracts with them—approximately 1.3 million people during 1981 (See Appendix B).

These figures are difficult to assess. There are obviously overlaps. Many who are on welfare use other services and are counted again. Some elderly people may use several services and be overcounted. Others may be eligible for services but not use them. But a very rough estimate would be that over 750,000 Massachusetts residents (excluding prisoners) were recipients of some form of public human service in 1981, or 13 percent of the total population. It cost approximately $2.7 billion to provide these services, with about one third of the costs reimbursed by federal money (see Appendix B).[12]

Cold calculations cannot capture the reality, however. It is also necessary to remember the human side of the demand for services. Every Christmas, the *Globe* Santa presents its sad appeals. But every day, each one of the 750,000 people counted above awakens, lives a life where the need is great and the resources limited, and faces a radio show or a newspaper headline proclaiming more budget cuts and "sacrifice." The following people were among those we met or heard about during the course of this study. They are typical of the people who will continue to use services in the 1980s:

Debbie M. has been paraplegic since a high school illness. She is now a single parent living alone. She receives SSI for herself and welfare for her child. Medicaid pays for her and her daughter's medical care. She makes use of job training and transportation services from Massachusetts Rehabilitation. At one point, depression and loneliness helped to create a drinking problem, but with the help of AA and counseling at a community mental health center Debbie is now in good spirits and attending school, with plans to become a rehabilitation counselor. She is also active in an advocacy group that fights for rights for the disabled.

Marie K. is a young Italian mother of two whose husband left after four years of drunkenly abusing her. She and the children (a boy, five, and a girl, two) are on AFDC. Medicaid pays for general family medical expenses and covers the cost of her son's hearing aid. Food stamps help provide food for the family. Marie went on welfare after a stay at a battered women's shelter, partially funded through public money. Her current plans are to apply for federally supported financial aid and to attend school at a community college next year while her son is in school. She plans to put her daughter in day care in her neighborhood while she earns her degree in computer programming. She is worried, however, that proposed workfare programs will cut short her chance for college.

Tom G. is a sixty-eight-year-old black man whose wife died two years ago. Although he worked all his life, many of his jobs were not covered by Social Security so his small Social Security payments are supplemented by SSI. He lives in a three-room apartment in Dorchester with his older sister. Both Tom and his sister make use of the elderly center and the lunch program in their area. Last winter, when his sister was ill, a homemaker came to help out. Tom's health is good, although Medicaid covers the cost of visits to the doctor for his arthritis.

Heather O. is an eighteen-year-old runaway. She was in DPW foster care as a child because of family problems. When she was back home she couldn't get along with her mother so she ran away. At sixteen she was declared a Child in Need of Services and sent to live in a group home. She liked this home and liked the Medicaid-funded medical care she received to correct a noticeable dental problem. When the home closed due to managerial and financial problems, Heather was angry and went back to the streets. Picked up for prostitution, she was turned over to DYS which placed her in a special program for girls where she was receiving career training as well as individual counseling.

Each of the people receiving services has a similar story. Some individuals have far greater need. Others only seek day care, counseling services, or food stamps. The services all receive are limited and none solve all the problems of those who receive them. But they allow each person to live, even to have some hope for his or her life, and almost all are available because the state and federal governments have made legal commitments to provide them.

Some of the people receiving services at the beginning of the 1980s will need services throughout the decade. Others will change their circumstances and stop needing services. The average woman is on welfare for less than 3.7 years. Many women go back and forth on welfare, because of the difficulty in keeping a job as a single parent, or because of emergency needs of their children. Some of the elderly will die; others will have greater needs and require greater services. (Tom or his sister, for example, could need a nursing home at some point.) If unemployment increases in Massachusetts there may be increased demand for food stamps or welfare. In short, there is no reason to think that major changes will take place to reduce the numbers of people seeking public services during the 1980s.

The current federal and state cutbacks and the changes in national philosophy have brought changes in the attitudes of some recipients, however. Like Debbie M., many are joining advocacy groups to organize, lobby, pressure, and demonstrate for their rights to continued care. Women on welfare, particularly, have been active with a strategy of demonstrations and public relations —especially using the radio and television talk shows. But elderly and disabled recipients have organized also. Their tone is less militant and lively than that of the welfare groups, but they too have created a presence in the agencies, the legislature, and the media.

All of this information suggests several questions for a historical analysis. Have the numbers changed? Are more or less people receiving services now than in the past? Have the types of services people use changed over time? How typical is the current level of consumer advocacy? What happened to similar groups in the past? Are people who need services treated better or worse than they used to be? Each of these questions is important, and we will return to them after examining our history and see what has been learned.

What services are provided and how are they organized?
As mentioned earlier, the Commonwealth of Massachusetts spends approximately $2.5 million on human services, not counting prisons and some medical-care programs. This money is spent on an astonishing variety of programs organized in a highly complex system. Most services are provided by agencies under the administrative directive of the Executive Office of Human Services (EOHS). Services for the elderly are delivered separately under the Executive Office for Elder Affairs. Housing services are included under the Executive Office of Communities and Development. Employment services are under the Office of Manpower Affairs. The best way to get a picture of the whole system is to portray it graphically, as we do in chart 1. Below, we will briefly summarize the major components of the current system in an attempt to provide a structured base for evaluating the many organizational changes that brought us to the present.

The two most powerful secretariats are Administration and Finance (A & F) and Human Services. Although A & F does not administer services, its financial oversight and regulatory policies have an important influence over the options available to human service administrators.

The Executive Office of Human Services is accountable for 42 percent of the state's spending, or $2.4 million in 1980 (see Appendix B for more information on state human service expenditures.) In the executive office itself, the secretary wields a great amount of informal and somewhat less formal power over the human service departments, although the major program expenditures are guided by federal and state guidelines that limit the Secretary's power. The secretary's office, then, calls meetings, appoints departmental commissioners, and exerts as much influence as possible over the direction of departmental policies. Proposed changes in federal policy may allow more state discretion in program and spending decisions and may enhance the power of EOHS.

The EOHS, situated in the State House, exhibits a highly professional and businesslike style, an atmosphere in sharp contrast to the dingy, double-knit demeanor in the Department of Public Welfare (DPW)—the largest department within the secretariat. DPW is responsible for 75 percent of human service funds. It administers those programs commonly known as welfare programs: Aid to Families with Dependent Children (AFDC), General Relief (GR), and Medicaid (MA). It also transfers the funds for Supplemental Security Income (SSI) to federal Social Security authorities. (See Appendix E for summaries of these major welfare programs.) These expensive programs provide the basic living allowances for poor children and their mother or unemployed father (AFDC), living expenses for unemployed adults (GR), or they allow for medical services (Medicaid) where the money actually goes to doctors, hospitals, pharmacists, and nursing homes. Poor elderly and physically disabled people receive SSI (a federal program administered by Social Security but supplemented with state funds), which provides a small living allowance. The department also operates a small Emergency Assistance program to cover fuel and other emergency costs for low-income families.

The amounts provided for families and individuals under SSI, GR, and AFDC are low, never taking people above the poverty level.[13] The department also determines eligibility for the Food Stamp program, which, however, is all federal (administered by the Agricultural Department), so only the administrative costs appear in the state's welfare budget. Food stamps, like Medicaid, are a benefit to poor people but do not provide cash assistance.

As of July 1980, the Department of Public Welfare was no longer responsible for social service programs. These are now provided by the Department of Social Services (DSS), which was instituted in July 1978. The new department now administers social services (under Title XX of the Social Security Act, the Children in Need of Services Program [CHINS] and child-welfare programs) and oversees the management of the contracts for social services awarded to other public and private agencies (70 percent of DSS's budget will go to contracted services provided outside the department). As was true under the Welfare Department, many DSS services—all except protective services and referral services—are provided primarily for low-income people, although there are some sliding fee scales available. The services include such programs as day care, foster care, homemaker and home services, recreation, transportation, residential services, alcoholism counseling, to name only a few. Most of the staff have come over from the Department of Public Welfare, although there are also many new young professionals in the central and local offices.

It is important to note that all the expensive programs administered by DPW and DSS (except General Relief) are heavily reimbursed by the federal government. In fact, for every dollar Massachusetts spends on income for an eligible AFDC family, the state gets fifty cents back from the federal government. Similarly, fifty cents on every dollar spent for Medicaid is returned. Social services are reimbursed at a rate of seventy-five cents on the dollar, although a federal ceiling in state allotments means that Massachusetts does not get paid back for all its service expenditures. Because reimbursement is conditional—that is, it is only awarded after money is spent and federal regulations governing the expenditures are met—the full cost of most welfare and social service programs must appear in the state budgets. This inflates the welfare budget and is often difficult to explain to the layperson—and even the lay-legislator.

The Department of Mental Health (DMH) is the second largest program in the secretariat, accounting for 16 percent of the human service expenditures. The department provides institutional care for the mentally ill (in state hospitals) and for the mentally retarded (in state schools). It also provides for community outpatient and residential care in smaller facilities for both groups. Special residential and out-patient programs are funded for the developmentally disabled, the drug dependent, older people, and children.

The department is now in the last phases of its deinstitutionalization program, which, due to political and budgetary opposition,

Chart 1

Human Service Programs in Massachusetts* 1980

Executive Office of:

Administration/Finance	Human Services	Elder Affairs
No delivery of service Can exercise important controls over human service spending	Department of Public Welfare AFDC—financial assistance GR — Medicaid—medical assistance oversees food stamp program other small financial assistance programs	Department of Elder Affairs Home Care Corporations Oversees other elderly service and planning programs supported by the Older Americans Act and Title XX
	Department of Mental Health Mental Hospitals Community Mental Health Mental Retardation Schools Developmental Disabilities programs	
	Department of Social Services* Title XX Child Welfare CHINS	
	Department of Public Health Clinics Licensing Alcoholism WIC Public Health	
	Department of Corrections Prisons Parole	
	Department of Youth Services	
	Office for Children	
	Veterans Services	
	Commission for the Blind	
	Rehabilitation Commission	
	Rate Setting Commission	

| Governor | ——————— | General Court |

Cabinet

Manpower Affairs	Communities/ Development	Educational Affairs	Other Non-Human Service Secretariats
Division of Employment Security	Public Housing oversight	766 special education program	Environmental Affairs
CETA-training and education services to smaller cities and towns (larger cities receive money directly from feds)	Rental Assistance	Adult Education	Consumer Affairs
			Energy Resources
			Transportation and Construction
			Public Safety

* The Department of Social Services began operation in July of 1980.
Source: Taken from data in Massachusetts Taxpayers Foundation—*State Budget Trends 1972–1981* (Boston, Mass.: 1980)

was recently slowed down from the goal of total shutdown. In 1980 the department hired 19,000 state workers to oversee a population of 6,400 in mental hospitals and state schools, as well as to provide community-based care. The thrust of both arms of the department has been to develop and expand community-based care but is shifting somewhat under budgetary constraints.

Other agencies in the secretariat account for only 11 percent of the human services spending—although many are in the public eye and give flavor to the meaning of human services. Here we will briefly list them and the services they provide.

The Department of Youth Services (DYS) spent $24 million in 1980 providing services for juveniles in trouble with the law. It provides community services such as group care, foster care, day and recreational programs. It also provides a set of secure facilities for youths deemed by the courts to be too violent to be treated in the community. Recently, the governor and the legislature have exerted pressure on DYS to expand its secure facilities.

The Office for Children (OFC) is not primarily a direct-service agency. It is an advocacy agency responsible for coordinating, evaluating, and setting standards for childrens' services. Its Help for Children system provides information to parents and social agencies. Otherwise, its Councils for Children plan and advocate for children but do not provide services themselves. OFC also sets licensing and evaluation standards for residential and day care programs. Its budget is small and there have been plans, thus far thwarted but gaining in momentum, to abolish it and disburse or eliminate its functions.

The Massachusetts Rehabilitation Commission (MRC) administers direct federal grants to provide vocational rehabilitation services to disabled citizens (except for the blind, who have their own commission). It provides counseling, guidance, and placement, sheltered workshops, training, transportation, and other direct services. State investment in MRC was approximately $5 million in 1981, but the agency also receives $20.5 million from the federal government to administer and deliver a range of services.

The Department of Public Health (DPH) has many general health responsibilities that are not considered social services. It oversees public health hospitals and community clinics, regulates standards of health-care facilities and prisons, and is responsible for the general public's health. Its Division of Alcoholism supports halfway houses which provide a range of social services. DPH is also involved in some family planning, women and children's preventive health programs, lead paint removal, and family health projects which do provide further direct human services to the poor. Funding cuts have recently diminished many department service programs and threaten to affect more in the future.

The remaining major service program outside the Human Services Secretariat is the Office of Elder Affairs. The secretary of Elder Affairs, a separate cabinet-level secretariat, is responsible for the Department of Elder Affairs (DEA), which is in turn responsible for all major service, planning, and advocacy programs for older citizens. The department receives substantial direct federal funding from the Older Americans Act, which supports certain central agency functions as well as the Area Agencies of Aging, senior centers, training programs, and an advocacy program. State and social service funds support twenty-seven private, nonprofit, Home Care Corporations which provide or contract for case management, information and referral, chore, homemaker, and transportation services. The Department of Elder Affairs received $45 million in state appropriations in 1980 and oversaw the expenditure of over $16.9 million in federal funds.

Two remaining service programs affect the poor in Massachusetts: housing and employment services. Unfortunately, these programs are quite separate from the other human services, a fragmentation that reflects federal funding patterns but that creates critical problems for clients and service workers. Both are associated with different federal agencies (Housing and Urban Development and the Department of Labor) and have very different guidelines and practices from the services treated here. Because they operate so independently from other services and are unfamiliar to many of the people we interviewed, we have made the reluctant decision not to consider them as a part of this study. But, perhaps, their very exclusion—when they represent such basic services to clients—is but another manifestation of the Circle Game.

Such an overview cannot help being overwhelming. One member of our research team described her reaction to a similar presentation with a response that seems to be quite common:

I can't stand it. There are too many programs, with too many things to do. How can I keep track of it all? Or see the connections? I feel like every time I think I understand it I hear about a whole new program, with new initials and new rules, which makes me think I don't know anything.

As was suggested in chapter 1, such a complex system does create confusion, and a need for historical background. Its current status suggests a number of questions. How did such a mixture of programs develop? Have they always been this way? How do agencies die or come to be created? In times of crisis, like the current budget situation, how have decisions been made? How are rivalries resolved among the different agencies? And what about the people who work in the system? Have they changed over the years? How important are individuals, secretaries, commissioners, or governors to the daily operations? Again, we will return to these questions later in the hope that our historical review begins to suggest some answers for the past which may help us in the 1980s.

Major current issues
A range of issues also defines the world of Massachusetts human services, issues with roots in the past which need to be understood.

The big issue is money. For the first few years of the 1980s, at least, money will be the most important consideration for human-service workers, administrators and clients. Federal budget cuts will force the state government to reduce programs. The effects of Proposition 2½ will create great pressure on the state to increase its local aid, in order to help local governments cover lost revenue.[14] Any attempt to shift the patterns of state spending must affect the human service programs that comprise almost half the state budget. Although, as can be seen in Appendix C, human service costs have remained level since 1976—when controlled for inflation—elected officials are insistent that service programs must face cuts, as well as show evidence of increased fiscal "efficiency" and better management.

Although, as we will see, cost concerns have always been critical issues facing human service programs, the magnitude of cuts facing Massachusetts is unprecedented. In the past, advocates rallied for more, or to keep one program. Commissioners worried over "level funding." The first years of the '80s promise yearly budget reductions of from 10 to 20 percent and massive layoffs, unless tax reform or other unexpected developments occur.

Such a financial climate creates both depression and hysteria within the system. It makes rational planning and evaluation of programs seem fruitless and it makes outsiders forget that there are other issues. But the other problems remain and create ongoing stress for workers and administrators alike.

Another current issue also has roots in the past, but is now felt with new urgency. The Reagan administration has a strong commitment to "getting the federal government off the backs" of state and local governments. This will be manifested in increased decision-making options at the local level, albeit coupled with reduced allocations. The state may find itself facing policy choices that have long been taken for granted, because they have been part of federal requirements. This may suggest reorganization of the state system of services, or shifting roles for professional and client advocacy groups. The prospects are intriguing, but frightening, as one advocate noted in the summer of 1981:

We have always argued for more local and state decision making, so it's hard to oppose this [new federal block-grant proposal]. But we're bound to have severe budget cuts, so the picture changes.

It's ironic that when they finally say they are giving us power, it's the "power" to decide how to cut needed services.

Another issue facing the state is one of how best to treat its welfare recipients. Facing economic hard times, officials admit that they wish to retreat from "overly generous" benefits to AFDC recipients. Their cry is to put welfare mothers to work, to limit welfare costs and to stop welfare fraud.[15] Such language has already provoked strong reaction among recipient and advocacy groups and is sure to remain on a highly vocal and emotionally charged public agenda for years to come.

Deinstitutionalization is another current issue that will continue to cause debate during the next years. The state has significantly reduced its institutionalized populations and created a widespread, and costly, system of community care. But professionals and advocates are divided about the benefits of the program as it has been conducted. So the 1980s will be a time of serious rethinking and refocusing on mental health—a process that will be made more difficult by budget cuts.[16]

The historical overview to follow will provide a sense of the background for these issues and may provide some suggestions about how they will (and should?) be resolved. Besides this quest for roots, however, perhaps the biggest questions our look backwards should address are: how did past patterns of service delivery help to create a climate where many residents of Massachusetts are willing, even eager, to make dramatic and critical cuts in every type of human service program? and are there any lessons from the past about how to respond to such cuts and such hostility?

If we can even begin to answer such questions we may have some hope for real progress in affecting future rounds of the Circle Game.

3 Up and Down and Around: 1966–1978

In such a structural review, human services in Massachusetts appear pretty well organized, nicely locked into separate categories and program priorities. There is a place for children's advocacy and a place for old people, one group to provide income maintenance and another to deliver rehabilitation services. It is almost too neat.

Indeed, it is too neat. When we look behind the broad organizational categories to the history of different programs we come away with another picture, of ever-changing, ever-shifting projects, priorities, and organizational agendas. This history gives us a sense of shifts and starts, reforms and new beginnings, which makes us distrust the clean, well-organized image put forward each year by official presentations of state government. One veteran administrator summed up the history of Massachusetts human service in an especially telling way:

It's like one of those magic boxes. You look in and you see all the colored pieces put together and they look really pretty. You turn it slightly and look again and you see the same pieces organized in a little different way. It's pretty still, but you start to wonder what's coming next. After you look a few more times, you start to feel a little crazy, like you see all the pieces but you don't know what's really there.

Beginnings of a System: Services in 1966

For many reasons, 1966 is an appropriate year to begin an inquiry into contemporary Massachusetts human services. It was the year that a Republican, John Volpe, captured the governor's office after four years of Democratic control. Volpe and his lieutenant governor, Francis Sargent, did not create campaign issues out of the need for changes or improvements in human services. Indeed, this was to be the last gubernatorial election in which the "welfare mess" and the "human service budget" were *not* major campaign questions. However, in a classic Massachusetts pattern of Republican governors and Democratic legislators working uneasily together to forge reforms, the next eight years were to see many planned and unplanned changes in Massachusetts state government, especially in the human service arena.[1]

Another reason for viewing 1966 as an important watershed is that it marked the beginning of public discussion about the proper organization of the state's welfare system. In December 1965, the National Study Service, a New York based social welfare research group, published its report, *Meeting the Problems of People in Massachusetts: A Study of the Massachusetts Public Welfare System.*[2] This ninety-eight page report was the result of an effort by the Welfare commissioner, Robert Ott, private social welfare professionals, and legislative leaders to launch a public campaign to redesign the structure of welfare programs in Massachusetts. The study did this, documenting in great depth the administrative, fiscal, and programmatic problems posed by the existing welfare structure.

It was not hard to see difficulties in the way welfare services were delivered in 1966. At that time, Massachusetts was one of the few states in the nation to retain a locally administered system of public welfare services. The Massachusetts Department of Public Welfare consisted of a commissioner and a small administrative staff of less than fifty people. Its main job was to see that federal matching funds for eligible programs (Aid to Families with Dependent Children, Old Age Assistance, and Disability Assistance) were properly routed to the 351 cities and towns and that state supports for such programs, and for General Relief, were being properly administered. A small medical assistance program for the elderly was also provided by cities and towns with state and federal assistance (see Appendix C for the programs administered by local cities and towns in 1966). State welfare officials promulgated certain guidelines and tried to guarantee that state and federal money was being spent appropriately. They were, however, uninvolved in the day-to-day delivery of welfare. As one state official remembered:

All we could do was to try to make sure nobody was giving the money away. We tried to push for proper procedures and documentation so that the feds would not be too unhappy. But we could not do anything about the *spirit* in which welfare was administered. We knew that some towns were patronizing or even downright hostile to clients but there was little or nothing we could do about anything like that.

The cities and towns considered welfare theirs and there was nothing we could do about it.

The state had "taken over" the administration of child welfare services in 1953, under the leadership of a younger Robert Ott, and had created a small statewide social work program, the Division of Child Guardianship (DCG), to deal with children and families needing protective services, foster care, or adoption. DCG was administered through regional offices.

In 1966, the DCG workers worked closely with local welfare workers who referred clients to them when they needed special services. DCG also worked with private social service agencies which provided 52 percent of the state's child welfare services (paid for on a case-by-case basis) for children needing assistance. If other AFDC families or elderly and disabled people needed non-income services they might be provided by local welfare offices that had small budgets for "social services."

This system left most poor people subject to the vagaries of town and city politics. Some cities developed large welfare systems, subject to city civil service rules and local political and patronage pressures. One hundred and eight small towns often had very small one-person welfare offices and highly personalized styles of welfare delivery. Welfare regulations for AFDC recipients allowed for a standard budget and then provided options for a wide range of supplementary increases for "special needs," subject to the discretion of the individual social worker. General Relief programs left the single adult poor person even more dependent on a social worker's preference.

Different cities and towns developed different patterns of informing recipients of available options. And within a city or town, different workers might vary widely in allocating benefits. Similarly, one family (or old person) might receive social services in one town and a family with similar problems might never hear of them in a welfare office a few miles away. One woman remembers it this way:

We were on welfare in Brockton and got next to nothing. My mother moved to Boston and we got special diet money for me and a new bedroom set and refrigerator. My mother thought things were really better until her first social worker left and another one came. He kept visiting our house and making my mother nervous looking for men, accusing her of taking money "under the table." She decided to move back to Brockton and one of the reasons was that she thought that even if they didn't give you much money there, at least they didn't bother you all the time.

Local officials admitted there were problems with the welfare system and differences between towns, but some initially argued that these reflected different local patterns. For many local administrators the answer was not, as the National Study Service suggested, a big state bureaucracy, which would, they argued, be "out of local control." Indeed, during the major discussions in the media and in the legislature over the next two years, no one seriously denied the problems found by the National Study Service. Debate centered only on the feasibility of following its recommendations. State officials and representatives of the larger cities and towns tended to favor the state takeover proposed by the report, as a way to make the system more consistent and efficient. Those who opposed it did so because they argued that the problem could best be solved locally, with more state assistance (see Appendix E for major recommendations of the study).

In short, welfare in Massachusetts in 1966 was a highly decentralized, largely hidden system. The Welfare budget was divided among each city's and town's allocation, so that only small central office and DCG expenses appeared as "welfare costs." While the total spent on welfare programs was, in fact, the largest state human service outlay, it was not viewed as such, but, rather, as part of local welfare expenditures. As one community advocate recalls, "As I remember, there was little agitation about 'welfare' in those days. We focused on the schools, or on health and housing, but welfare didn't become important until later."

In 1966, central office personnel in DPW were traditional social workers with little management background—or interest in the "business" aspects of the system. The Division of Child Guardianship dealt with the "toughest" cases in the state and was seldom in the limelight. The agency exhibited all the problems found in the National Study Service review, to be sure, but they were old, well-known problems with which, it seemed, almost everyone had become quite comfortable. It was only when medical costs expanded as a result of the new Medicaid program (begun in response to federal initiative in 1966) and when welfare recipients began to make noise and trouble at local welfare offices, that strong enough pressures were generated to force bureaucratic change. By late 1966, both of these new forces were felt by bureaucrats and legislators.

A final reason why 1966 seems a crucial starting point is because during the year the legislature passed a bill that was to set the pattern for major changes in mental health programs in the state. Massachusetts has long been, since the days of Dorothea Dix in the late 1800s, a state that prided itself on its mental health programs and reforms. It is the home of a large number of distinguished, and traditional, psychiatrists and psychiatric social workers. Furthermore, its programs for the retarded had been national models in the early years of this century. In 1966, the Commonwealth spent 8 percent of its budget to house more than 26,000 people in state mental health hospitals and schools for the retarded. The staff who cared for these people were the largest group of state workers. Indeed, much more than welfare, in 1966 it was mental health and retardation programs that were thought of as the state's "human services." [3]

However, both nationally and locally, there were pressures for change. The development of new drugs and new forms of treatment in the 1950s had led to increased public pressure for change by the relatives of patients and by many professionals. The increasing costs of institutional care and the problems with staffing and administering large facilities had led to calls for "community care" and an end to "warehousing" the mentally ill and retarded.[4] In 1963 the Congress passed the Community Mental Health and Retardation Centers Act which provided the possibility of federal funds for building and implementing community facilities. Thus, in 1966, after a study of the feasibility of community care in Massachusetts, the legislature passed Chapter 735, the Comprehensive Mental Health and Retardation Services Act. This reorganized the old Massachusetts Department of Mental Health, called for the establishment of citizens' boards, and created a complex regional and area structure. It mandated that the department move toward community care facilities for both the mentally ill and retarded.

The legislation did not push for immediate change but it did provide a strong new direction for a major state agency. DMH at the time employed more than 16,000 people, 1,000 of whom were in one hospital alone. The department was headed by psychiatrists and closely tied to the academic psychiatric community in Boston. Its commissioners were not viewed as political appointees but as professionals. So it is no wonder that, however dramatic the new legislation might be, it took awhile for the Massachusetts mental-health system to respond.[5]

In 1966, only a few of the other pieces that currently make up the Massachusetts service system were in place. For delinquent youth there were Youth Service Boards. State training "schools" for almost 1,000 youth—modeled on prisons—were overseen by

John Coughlin, long-time head of the Division of Youth Services, within the state Department of Education. While there were rumblings of professional discontent with the treatment in these state schools, little was publicly aired. The Massachusetts Rehabilitation Commission was operating much as it does today, with substantial federal funding. There was no special department for older citizens or for children. Each state agency director reported directly to the governor and there was little or no upper-level coordination or communication (see chart 2). While a welfare worker might be in contact with the Youth Board or with the area state hospital, there was only minor state-level coordination. Private agencies kept to themselves—except for those that dealt with abused, neglected, or foster children. These worked with DCG to coordinate financial and legal arrangements for families, and were reimbursed on a case-by-case basis.

Clients were still needy, as the National Study Service revealed:

Mrs. O., mother of four young children, is legally separated from her husband. This action followed a stormy marriage, with Mr. O. being an alcoholic and physically abusive to Mrs. O. Following the separation, his failure to support regularly resulted in several court complaints after which he would get drunk and again become physically abusive. He finally deserted the family, and his current whereabouts are unknown. She is trying to support her family by working, but has just lost her second job because of frequent illness.

Mrs. G. is 61 years old. She is a widow who supported herself by domestic labor until four years ago. Her two grown children, both married, are trying to provide for her but their increasing responsibilities for their growing families have made this almost impossible. They do pay the rent, but cannot do more—particularly in the face of ever mounting medical needs. She is suffering from diabetes, gout, arteriosclerosis and has been told by her physician that she must not try to work. Her application for Disability Assistance has been turned down twice by the State Medical Review Team because she is not permanently and totally disabled. She is living on a grossly inadequate General Relief grant.

Mary, age 15, is mentally retarded. Her mother has been in a state mental hospital since shortly after Mary was born. There is no knowledge of her father. After six years in a series of foster homes, Mary was sent to live with her aunt who has three children of her own. The psychologist says Mary's retardation may be due in part to emotional problems. The aunt has sufficient income to care for her and wishes to help her, but she wants someone to advise her as problems arise.

The study commented on these and other cases it cited by noting:

If all these [218,000] adults and families and children now known to the welfare departments were brought together in one place, they would populate a city larger than Worcester. If they actually did live in one large city, everyone would be aware of their existence. In reality, however, they are only 4.1 percent of the more than five million people in this large Commonwealth, and they are largely lost to sight. . . . Except to their relatives, to some people with whom they do business and to members of the various helping professions, these people are likely to be nameless, faceless and unnoticed. . . .

Nevertheless, they are there—the poor and the not so poor, the young and the old, the sick and the well. They suffer, they cry and sometimes they strike back.[6]

The next few years in Massachusetts were to change this anonymity. Although the general public and the legislators may not have become more sensitive to individual needs such as those described above, they were forced to become aware of the existence of inadequate welfare programs and the anger and desperation which may be expressed when participants in the system "strike back."

Rebellion, Reform and, Reaction: 1966–1970

Those were the days. People were willing to fight and we wouldn't put up with much. We would go to the welfare offices with somebody who hadn't been able to get anything from her worker. Next thing we knew she would be found eligible—for special diets, children's beds, a washing machine, everything.
We didn't always win, but we always fought for what we thought was right. And lots of workers and even supervisors helped us. Even those who were against us kept pretty quiet. [Welfare rights organizer]

The popular image of the late 60s is one of marches, protests, and demands for rights—civil rights, rights to resist the draft, women's rights, welfare rights. The image still contains much power and veracity. Not that everyone marched, certainly, but a climate of energy and protest was created. There was enough civil disorder in the nation's cities—including Boston—to frighten officials, especially welfare officials. As Frances Fox Piven and Richard A. Cloward have argued, this threat of disorder helped to justify the expansion of services to placate rioters.[7] The new War on Poverty, with its Community Action Projects, its Head Start and Model

Cities programs gave poor areas a means to by-pass traditional state agencies and a tool to help them push for more benefits. The expanding, generally healthy economy made concessions seem bearable. Professionals devised plans for expanded services that built upon the demands of protesters (and provided jobs for professionals). So the period from 1966 to 1970 was generally one of human service expansion, innovation, and development, with the tacit support even of Massachusetts governors, according to one high-level official:

Volpe didn't care. He was out of the state, running for vice president or seeking a position with Nixon. But he did want order and harmony so he supported concessions by omission. Sargent was even softer. He not only wanted harmony but he sometimes listened to the protesters and was even swayed, on political and moral grounds, by some of their arguments. So the stage was set for professional and client advocates to push hard, and they did.

The state takeover of welfare

After the publication of the National Study Service Report in December 1965, service advocates went to work, persuading legislators and other professionals of the need for a statewide system. Influential legislators were won over. Three major factors convinced opponents to support what all recognized would be a costly takeover: (1) the increasing numbers of AFDC recipients statewide; (2) the pressure of welfare rights organizing on local cities and towns; (3) the sharp growth, with predictions of even greater increases, in Medicaid costs.[8]

There are many explanations for the state (and national) increases in the AFDC rolls during this period. Some see the increase as reflecting the changed status of women, who were gradually becoming more able to work outside the home, to divorce, and to raise their children without men. Others see improving benefits and reduced stigma as attracting more eligible people to apply. Some attribute the expansion to domestic migration which saw southern blacks moving north and west to states where the financial benefits were greater and the social stigma less. And an important argument is made that civil rights and welfare rights agitation led to expanded eligibility and benefits, as the system tried to quell discontent by offering increased social programs.[9] For our purposes here, we see the increases as resulting from the interaction of all these factors, perhaps catalyzed by the publicity given to welfare rights struggles. And, whatever the causes, we find

Chart 2

Human Service Programs in Massachusetts 1966 *

Department of Mental Health	Department of Public Welfare	Department of Education	Department of Public Health
State Hospitals for the Mentally Ill	Division of Child Guardianship (regionally administered)	Youth Service Boards	Public Health
State Schools for the Retarded		Division for the Blind	Alcoholism
	Small administrative staff to oversee local cities and towns who received direct state aid to supply AFDC; GR; OA; DA; medical assistance and other small financial assistance programs		

* Source: Comptroller's Division, December, 1966

similar results—local cities and towns found themselves with larger welfare rolls, more demanding clients, more paper work, bigger budgets, and more public scrutiny than ever before. Increasingly, it became difficult even for small towns to run their welfare programs in an orderly fashion.

Welfare organizing in Boston, Springfield, and other cities made running welfare offices a less simple task. Since 1965, when Mothers for Adequate Welfare (MAWs) was founded in Boston, women on AFDC, many of them black and influenced by the civil rights movement, had been organizing to help women gain their full benefits and to push local departments to give recipients all the benefits to which they were entitled. With the help of sym-

| Governor | ———————————— | General Court |

Executive Office
for Administration/Finance

Office of Commissioner
of Administration

Comptroller's
Division

Purchasing
Agent's Division

Department of
Corrections

Massachusetts
Rehabilitation
Commission

Commission
on Aging
Research/Policy

Department
of Labor/
Industries

Division of
Employment
Security

Department of
Commerce/
Development

Elderly housing
Public housing

(Other non-human service departments reporting directly to Governor:
Agriculture, Banking and Insurance,
Civil Service and Registration, Corporations and Taxes, Metropolitan
District Commission, Natural Resources, Public Safety, Public Utilities, Public Work, Miscellaneous
commissions boards, etc.)

pathetic social workers, MAWs—and later, the National Welfare
Rights Organization—ran "diet clinics" to help recipients learn
how to receive extra money for special diets as well as money and
vouchers for other special needs. Groups of women, armed with a
knowledge of their rights, would go to welfare offices in Boston
and other cities, using tactics aimed at making it difficult to turn
them down.[10]

The regulations, as we have seen, allowed for greater worker
discretion in the assignment of benefits. Welfare rights chapters
were, therefore, often highly successful in getting maximum allocation of benefits as standard practice. In Boston, many workers
were supportive of welfare organizers. In other cities, some work-

ers were supportive and others were willing to go along. A union veteran of the period recalls the pressures:

Everything was crazy. More and more people were applying for welfare. You never knew when twenty women would come in with your client yelling at you and demanding their rights. Even if you weren't sympathetic you quickly learned to provide everything the law allowed, and your supervisors supported you, just to keep the peace.

And a local official also remembers the tensions:

Before the mid-sixties, welfare was almost a family operation in our town. We knew most of the families and they knew us. Then the numbers starting going up. We didn't have real protests, but we did have more people being pushy for whatever they thought they deserved. And we all knew what happened in Boston. So after a while the idea of the state taking over welfare didn't seem so bad, especially with Medicaid.

Medicaid was the final pressure that led local officials and state legislators to support a state takeover of welfare. Passed by Congress in 1965 as Title XIX of the Social Security Amendment, Medicaid provided 50 percent federal reimbursement for most medical expenditures for indigent individuals of most categories—the aged, disabled, AFDC, even the working poor with high medical expenses. In 1966, Massachusetts initiated the program, with all the benefits allowed, as a replacement for the small Medical Assistance program that had covered emergency and critical medical costs for the indigent elderly. The new program required a complex billing and eligibility system and the development of a complicated vendor payment system. Many cities and towns were simply unable to set up appropriate administrative procedures for coping with the new program. Hospitals, doctors, druggists, and nursing homes went unpaid for months, even years. Procedures varied from town to town. Medical establishments often had to have as many as four or five different procedures for patients from different towns.

Costs rose dramatically from 1966 to 1968 and all observers saw no early end to the increase (Appendix B). As one state Medicaid official observed: "The cities and towns were in over their heads. If anything forced the state takeover, it was the necessity for a state Medicaid program."

Yet, although enabling legislation was introduced earlier, it wasn't until a typical Massachusetts political crisis took place in December 1967 that a final decision was made. As Margaret Weinberg described in *Managing the State*, Kevin White played a final midwife role:

There were strong political pressures at work to make the General Court pass the legislation. Kevin White, the Secretary of State, had just been elected Mayor of Boston. John Davoren, the Speaker of the House, was anxious to be named Secretary, but White, who was stepping into the job as chief executive of the City of Boston, with the largest welfare population in the state, refused to yield the Secretary's job until the Legislature passed the takeover bill.[11]

When the legislature did decide, its approach was comprehensive. The state took over all local costs, including the total responsibility for General Relief—of which it had previously only paid a small fraction. Local welfare officials were allowed to become state employees. Fearful of increased operating costs, the legislature was reluctant to allocate increased planning funds or administrative supports to implement the new system. So the official takeover, which occurred on July 1, 1968, was traumatic. The new department was overwhelmed just by the task of centralizing and coordinating all the varying systems and methods it inherited, to say nothing of collecting information into a computer system. Robert Ott, the commissioner since 1963, was admittedly in a "management nightmare."

Such administrative problems were only heightened by increasing pressure from welfare rights groups. Now facing only one agency instead of 351, one commissioner and a newly responsible governor, welfare rights and professional advocacy groups were able to concentrate their pressure. Governor Sargent faced welfare mothers in the State House, Commissioner Ott was pressured at his office and his home. They demanded better benefits, fuller services, humane job programs and the control of "welfare lawlessness" among hostile workers unwilling to grant full benefits.

The new department was ill-equipped to deal with the pressure. Old legislative friends abandoned the commissioner, wanting an end to the agitation and also, by 1970, wanting to control welfare costs, which suddenly seemed so high now that they all appeared in one budget line item, and as Medicaid costs soared. The department also had to negotiate the first statewide union contract, another unfamiliar task. As one former union official remembers:

The department was under siege. Administratively, they could barely operate, they were so understaffed. They didn't even know who was on welfare, not to mention who worked for the department or who were their Medicaid vendors. Welfare-rights groups were always around. We negotiated the best contract we've ever had with them and I know it's because they were so overwhelmed.

In June 1970, Commissioner Ott resigned. In August, Governor Sargent hired Steven Minter (a black social worker and administrator from Cleveland, Ohio) to head the department. Minter's mandate was to clean up administratively and to handle the dissent so that, in the words of one high-level official, "the governor didn't have to read about welfare mothers at the State House over breakfast every morning."

Mental health reorganizes
During this period, the Department of Mental Health was responding to its own reorganization, enacted in 1966, as noted earlier. A new commissioner, Milton Greenblatt, was appointed in 1967, with a commitment to develop "community services." For the department this did not mean rapid deinstitutionalization. Rather, it involved organizing the forty area offices of mental health and seven regional offices, which were mandated by the legislature. Local area citizens' boards were established, and controversy grew over their role and power.

By the late sixties, advocacy groups were beginning to pressure the Department of Mental Health too. More professional and less vociferous than welfare rights groups, they began to put increasing pressure on the department to improve conditions in the state schools for the retarded and the state hospitals. The courts were used to seek legal remedies and force the department to provide better care, especially for children, and to place more patients in the community, where possible.

Even by 1970, however, these pressures were still muted. The department remained relatively stable, with its large numbers of state employees still staffing huge state institutions. It remained dominated by psychiatrists and the medical community, even as it made its slow plans, pushed by court mandates for deinstitutionalization (the first halfway house for retarded children opened in Somerville in 1968). The shift toward decentralization and area offices was also slow and careful. Indeed, it would have been difficult to look at DMH in 1970 and predict that in eight years it would be barreling toward full deinstitutionalization, an activist among local and state service agencies, and the acknowledged leader of human service departments in the state.

Youth program reform

As noted earlier, delinquent youth were incarcerated in state training schools until the late sixties. "Stubborn children" whose parents could not control them—although they had committed no crimes—were often cared for in such schools also. In 1966 an HEW report strongly criticized the prisonlike atmosphere of these schools and urged a more diversified, service-oriented approach to the care of the nearly 1,000 youths under state care.[12]

In 1969, professionals and youth advocates used the report to achieve the passage, with the governor's strong support, of legislation creating a Department of Youth Services, abolishing the local youth service boards and the old Division of Youth Services within the Education Department. The Director of Youth Services since the 1950s resigned and the first commissioner of the new agency was named. Jerry Miller, an audacious and activist social worker and corrections official, was appointed with the support of youth advocates who wanted new approaches to delinquency and troubled youth. His mandate was to reorganize and restructure.

By 1970, Miller's approaches had already begun to loosen the atmosphere in the state schools—by allowing longer hair and street clothes—and had set him in opposition to many of the "old guard" within the department. Under his leadership, the top administrators within the agency began searching for other models for the rehabilitation of youth. Within a few years their quest was to produce the most thorough reform of a human service program to take place during the decade.

Emerging issues

Advocacy abounded. Where there was an agency to pressure, professional and community advocates pressured. When there was no agency, advocates demanded one. This period saw an increase in groups organized to protect the interests and rights of children and of the elderly. In both areas, professionals and nonprofessionals united to convince the state to pay more attention to their constituencies.

Another theme of advocacy groups was "community care." Through the Taskforce on Children Out of School, advocates for children exposed the neglect of Boston's handicapped children by the Boston schools. The call was for full service in the community. Older people, led by advocate Frank Manning (who later became president of the Massachusetts Association of Older Americans), were demanding that more attention be paid to elderly citizens.

Although both groups demanded more attention from the state, they shared a concern that new programs allow for decentralization, a theme that would continue to affect human services throughout the 1970s.

In 1968, the State Planning Agency proposed the restructuring of state government into a cabinet system. Governor Sargent, his advisers, and the legislators adopted this proposal as a way to limit the programs that reported directly to the governor and to make the budget, personnel, and planning processes of the state bureaucracy more efficient. When those plans were passed, they created a cabinet of ten secretariats with limited power to oversee and organize the activities of the agencies within them. The Executive Office of Human Services emerged as the largest, covering almost all the major human service areas. A secretariat for Elder Affairs was added, under pressure from the elderly advocates, and plans began for the creation of a special children's agency. Slated to begin in 1971, the new cabinet system not only promised to provide for more cooperation and communication among state human service agencies, but it also embodied a stated commitment to some of the advocacy and community-based ideas of the human service constituency. One official remembers:

The reorganization was a mixed bag. As government grew it was clear that everyone could not report to the governor and that we needed more coordination among departments. So, it was probably necessary. It also allowed the state to say that it was responding to the advocacy groups and heeding the call for better government. On the other hand, in reality, the restructuring actually put another level of government between the governor and the advocacy groups and many people resented that.

Restructure and Retreat: 1970–1974

In 1971 the secretariat system began. The first secretary of Human Services was Peter Goldmark, a young "whiz kid" from Mayor Lindsay's New York City government. Goldmark's office, initially consisting of himself and one staff member, had the job of coordinating the tasks of the powerful, entrenched Welfare, Mental Health, Public Health and Corrections Departments, without exerting any line authority over their activities. Rather than fight the departments on most issues, Goldmark's strategy was to build up the program management capacity of his office and to become useful to the departments so that they would follow his policy directions. He also worked on plans for Phase II reorganization which was to give more power to the secretariats and allow them, according to the legislative proposal, "to establish and enforce general policies and standards of quality, cost and effectiveness." [13]

The struggle to achieve Phase II reorganization, which was never passed, combined with other departmental restructurings to make the second Sargent administration a time of intense attention to organizational patterns. In harmony with federally supported, nationwide efforts to coordinate and integrate services, the planners proceeded. At the same time consumer militance was declining, especially in welfare but also in other areas. And by 1973, the state economy had begun to sag, providing for a new, less supportive climate for human services.

Welfare under Minter

Steven Minter's first task was to deal with the welfare rights advocates. There were many structural ways in which this was accomplished, as well as many social forces outside the department that contributed to the decline in militancy. However, Minter's own style was a significant factor. He was unflappable at the hearings and meetings that allowed advocates to state their case. In the words of one militant, he was

a wet blanket. You could yell and he wouldn't say or do anything. Of course it wasn't just him. It was the strategy of the flat grant and the times, but it *was* a smart move to install a cool black man as commissioner, instead of the other guy [Ott] who got mad and wanted everybody to agree that he was doing all he could.

The first administrative task of the period was the installation of a flat grant to replace many of the special-needs categories that were the source of discrepancies in budgets. The flat grant was a means by which all recipients received an extra check four times a year, to cover special clothing, holiday and family-maintenance needs. Although at first a number of special-benefit categories remained, the program (actually planned and ready for implementation before Minter's arrival) did address equity concerns and, not incidentally, reduced the effectiveness of the advocacy strategy for welfare rights groups. The proposals were fought, but to no avail. And, over the next four years, the number of special needs for which recipients could receive money or vouchers decreased, as budget tightening was called for and as militance declined.

An important change, with long-range expectations, took place in AFDC during this period: welfare mothers were expected to work. Although not seriously implemented until later, a federal amendment was passed in 1967 which established the principle that women with children over age six were expected to work, and not only collect welfare. The Work Incentive Program (WIN) mandated job training or work as a means to reduce financial dependence. Special formulas were created to allow women to keep some of their earnings before their checks were reduced and some arrangements were available to cover child care and other work expenses. However, the federal government had loose guidelines and in the crazy, post-takeover years the program was little developed or enforced.

But new federal pressures to "tighten up" on nonworking recipients began to change the picture. By the early 1970s, the Work Incentive Program became a paradoxical fact of life for Massachusetts welfare recipients. One mid-level official explained:

When WIN was first started it was called WIP—work incentive program. You can imagine how the advocacy groups used that. They had great leaflets with cartoons of women being whipped. But even after it was changed to WIN, it was still a problem. It had to be jointly administered with DES [Division of Employment Security] and that was hard. It was supposed to allow for training but there wasn't much for decent jobs and there weren't many jobs to put people in. So it was there, but often ignored. Sometimes it was used punitively. If a worker didn't get along with her client, she would make her register for WIN. It was, and still is, a mess.

Indeed, most recipients interviewed did not feel that WIN was a very active program during these years. One woman's response was typical:

When my youngest was seven my worker reminded me that I had to register with WIN. I went down there, talked to the lady for thirty minutes, signed something and never heard from them again until I went looking for money to help me out with school expenses.

The pressures of coordinating with DES, keeping track of eligible women, and finding appropriate training or placement made WIN a low priority under Minter. Indeed, the largest attention WIN received was when a national amendment was proposed by Senator Talmadge in 1972, which would have forced women with children over three to work, even at low-paying public jobs. Advocacy groups rallied, spoke at local hearings, and were a part of a general effort to defeat the worst aspects of the measure. Otherwise WIN was just a program that would be mentioned to legislators and welfare critics as a "positive step," but it did not receive significant attention until later in the decade.

The early 1970s saw the emergence of other issues that were to consistently plague the department, and its clients, throughout the 1970s: fraud and error rate. In 1972 there was a burst of legislative and media concern about welfare fraud and there was talk of a "fraud squad" of welfare lawyers to end this problem. Little ever came of such efforts—because poor recordkeeping made fraud difficult to detect and because there was probably less serious recipient fraud than assumed by the public.[14] However, the threat of fraud squads was a means to keep people off the rolls or generally fearful of "causing trouble" because, as one recipient reported,

the AFDC budgets are so low you can't live on them without some help. Lucky women have family or friends who offer support, like the free use of a car or extra money. Others must take short-term jobs now and then to pay for a fuel bill or for Christmas toys. If you report this they deduct so much that it is not worth doing, so you work for a month here, a few weeks there, and you hope you don't get caught.

Workers were often blamed for recipient fraud. Therefore, the waves of public concern about it, and about worker "error rates," also served to make workers more cautious, more legalistic. One union official discussed the connection between increased administrative pressure about fraud and error rates and decreased worker support for clients:

Back in the sixties, early seventies, a worker was rewarded by clients and supervisors for saying "yes," for doing as much as she could for the client, within the rules. Now all the pressure from above comes for you to say "no"—you aren't suspected of being "soft"; you don't even have as many forms to fill out, if you deny something. It makes a big difference.

It started with the sporadic talk about fraud and error rate and just got worse. Gradually workers became afraid to believe anybody—they might be helping them commit fraud, or be themselves committing an error, horror of horrors. So workers began demanding more documents, being more suspicious—even when the client was clearly disorganized—and grew more fearful of breaking the rules. Within such an environment, it does not take long for workers to forget that they ever saw themselves as helping people get what they need.[15]

From 1972 until 1974, however, public legislative concern over fraud and error rates rose and fell depending upon who was on the welfare "beat" of the local newspaper or upon which legislator received an irate phone call. There was little systematic attention by administration or the governor's office regarding these matters. They were more concerned with trying to get the payroll centralized and computerized as well as trying to pay the Medicaid vendors on time, central tasks that were not really accomplished until almost the end of the Minter term in office.

On January 1, 1974, a significant change took place in the programs administered by Welfare. The elderly (OA) and disabled (DA) welfare categories were transferred to the new, federally funded Supplemental Security Income (SSI) program administered by the Social Security Office. Compared with other states this transition was administered with remarkable smoothness, commentators note. Lists of recipients and their status were sent to Social Security officials and clients were informed of their new program identification. While there was some confusion (especially for the disabled, regarding standards of their eligibility), the shift meant that almost overnight the department lost over 88,000 clients. One mid-level administrator commented:

It was almost like, after coping with the takeover, it was nothing to get rid of a few thousand cases. The department had never been too attentive to the elderly or disabled anyway. One day they were just gone and life in the offices went on almost as if nothing had happened.

The state continued to provide supplements to the basic SSI payment, to cover Medicaid costs, and to provide social services for SSI recipients. And some workers did take notice:

I missed my elderly caseload. They were a relief from the complex troubles of my AFDC folks. I felt like they were glad to see me (that was back in the days when we did a lot of visiting) and even though some people were sort of sad, visiting them still made me feel like I was doing something worthwhile, not just snooping around for evidence of fraud or child abuse, like with AFDC.

In 1974, the food stamp program was initiated statewide in Massachusetts replacing a haphazard system of surplus-food distribution. Welfare staff were involved in the planning of the change and in determining eligibility. Although not a major department function, the presence of the program did, in the words of one worker,

contribute to the sense that it was pretty good to be on welfare. A lot of workers would begin to feel that recipients could get food stamps *and* Medicaid *and* social services—that being poor wasn't so bad as it used to be. Of course, with inflation it wasn't really true, but I think that workers —and the general public—began to be less sympathetic after food stamps came in.

During the Minter administration the Medicaid program slowly began to come under control, although costs continued to rise. Central office staff were gradually increased and billing procedures were standardized—if not speeded up. The last Medicaid director under Minter, Mel Scovell, was more aggressive than his predecessors in negotiating with hospitals, nursing homes, and doctors. He also fought for qualified staff, and, in the words of one official, "he established the principle that Medicaid was an important part of the department and that it required trained staff with more specialized skill than other areas. Before Mel, many people in the department hadn't really thought that it took a different kind of effort to run Medicaid."

Social services changed dramatically during this period, although not as a direct result of serious administrative attention. Three major developments were "allowed to occur," in the words of one official, which ultimately meant important changes in how social services were viewed in the Commonwealth. First, soon after Minter's arrival, the department began to follow the lead of other states like Illinois, California, and New York and started purchasing social services for clients from private providers. Up until this time, as we have seen, the Commonwealth used its social services money (funded under Title IV of the Social Security Act, at 75 percent reimbursement) to provide protective, foster care and some other family-maintenance services itself or from a few private, established service providers. These agencies were recognized vendors who would be reimbursed for services referred to them on a case-by-case basis. Now the department began to expand its notion of acceptable services and to use the option of privately donated funds to provide the 25 percent match needed for federal reimbursement. Under this system, private agencies would donate funds to a state account which would then serve as the state's matching funds. Then the agency would receive three times the amount donated to run programs for eligible AFDC, elderly, and disabled clients.

The purchase of service and donated-funds approach had many advantages, according to one high-level official:

It allowed us to increase services without expanding state workers or even costs very much. It also kept the old-line social workers from gaining the power and status that they would have received if we had expanded direct state services. Finally, it allowed the department—which was saddled with more serious administrative problems elsewhere—to do something about services without a lot of thought or careful planning.

Thus services expanded but the department itself continued to provide mainly protective services and traditional child welfare services of adoption and foster care.

Since 1969, all states had been under federal mandate to separate service functions and staff from payments functions and staff. This innovation resulted from a long series of professional debates about the negative effect on services (such as family counseling, protective services) when the service worker also dealt with clients' income problems. Massachusetts had ignored this directive since its inception, primarily because of other administrative priorities but also out of some fear that there were, as some opponents of separation worried, "too few services to separate." [16]

By 1973, federal pressure increased, however, and the department began to suffer penalties for its failure to comply. In the summer of 1974, workers took civil service tests and by the end of the year, the functions were officially separated with service workers in different areas and sometimes even different offices from payment workers. However, the workers and administrators interviewed agreed, as one administrator commented, that "Yes, workers were separated and so were basic functions. But the planning and leadership which would have made 'services' and 'payments' feel like separate activities, with definite goals and identities, never really happened. Everyone still felt like a welfare worker."

The final service change under Minter was the passage of the Children in Need of Services (CHINS) legislation in 1973. Previously children in trouble who hadn't committed crimes could only be judged "stubborn children" and handled mainly through DYS (or sometimes through Welfare, if family members were recipients). Following national patterns, the Children in Need of Services legislation "decriminalized" these children (often runaways, or the victims of neglect and abuse) and laid their care clearly within the mandate of the Welfare Department's social services unit.[17]

All of these changes took place during four years of worsening state economy, of an increasing public climate of hostility to public services, and of declining recipient militance. Costs continued to expand, but more slowly than before. New ventures were attempted but they increasingly had to justify themselves by their efficiency as much as by their response to need.

The changing roles of mental health

From 1970 until 1974 the Department of Mental Health, often reluctantly, began to make strides into the world of innovative service delivery. In 1970, the Mental Health Reform Act restricted admissions policies for mental hospitals. By 1971, law suits were being pressed that demanded better care in the state schools. Area advisory boards were continuing to push for more power. In 1972, the report *Suffer the Children* was published by the Massachusetts Taskforce on Children Out of School (now Massachusetts Advocacy).[18] This report decried the lack of programs for the mental health needs of children. The authors quickly became engaged in a battle with Commissioner Greenblatt, who first tried to suppress the document, then denounced it, and finally refused to respond until forced to do so by Secretary Goldmark. In the words of one official, this interchange had lasting effects on the department:

Greenblatt was a professional. He couldn't deal with muckraking amateurs. When he (and the department) did not receive support in the face of *Suffer the Children*, he and some other psychiatrists in the department were crushed. On top of the court cases it was just too much. It meant to all of them that they were really going to have to deal with the public and advocates and administrators about issues, rather than relying on their "expertise." Greenblatt was not the only one who couldn't take it. And, unlike Greenblatt, some of them stayed in the department.

Greenblatt left in 1973 and was replaced, after a long search characterized by tensions among local mental health leaders and human service officials. The new commissioner was Robert Goldman, a California psychiatrist whose most recent San Francisco work had been to develop community-based and controlled mental health services. Goldman was a testy, tough individual who pushed hard on the bureaucratic forces within the department and against the traditional private mental health institutions. Under his short tenure a sense of energy for change was created, and some deinstitutionalization of state hospitals and schools did take place (although many complained that nursing homes and expanded Medicaid costs were too often the beneficiaries of this early effort).[19] Under Goldman's influence, DMH began the delicate negotiations with Welfare that were necessary if ex-patients were to use Medicaid and social service dollars to purchase their community-based services.

During this period, too, the area offices of Mental Health became more active and expansive in defining community mental health. While some remained the quiet, carpeted, out-patient mental health clinics of the past, many others—with the support of the commissioner—became involved in local community schools, housing projects, and alternative services. Thus they created an activist presence that had never before been associated with Mental Health.

The main image of the Department of Mental Health during this period was supplied by a twenty-year veteran mental health nurse:

Those were the days when you never knew what was going to happen. One day the old commissioner was under attack and was fighting back. Then he was gone and the message was to decentralize. The mental health and retardation people weren't speaking to each other. A new commissioner came who scared a lot of people with his tough-guy attitude. He talked a good game and said he wanted community services and people out of the hospitals but nobody knew how to deal with him. It was a crazy time with lots of rumors about everything.

Deinstitutionalizing youth services

By early 1971, Commissioner Miller and his key aides had begun to despair of gradual reform for the state training schools.[20] His experience with the staff in those institutions convinced him that if change was to come it would be through more drastic measures. He began exploring alternative means of funding community-based programs. For example, Miller looked to DARE, Inc. (founded in 1967) to become one of the first private programs to assume state contracts and provide the bulk of state-funded, community-based care for young people. Using state money, some special federal funds and some Welfare social services money, DYS began rapidly to empty the state institutions without an official order to close them. Staff were left with dwindling populations as their charges were moved to group homes, halfway houses and individual foster care. By 1972, the DYS population was 95 percent deinstitutionalized. Miller could then argue for closing essentially empty schools and replacing them with small "therapeutic communities" staffed by young, committed, nonprofessionals.

Such rapid change was not without its costs, however. Staff and many administrators felt that Miller was endangering public safety with "naive" hopes for rehabilitation outside of locked facilities. They were joined by influential criminal-justice professionals who stressed that some, if not all, the youths under DYS care were dangerous and uncontrollable. This concern over secure facilities, and exposés of lack of controls over the contracted services, finally led to Miller's resignation. This event, in one upper-level administrator's words, seemed

... inevitable. He emptied the schools but he couldn't lead, retrain, or redesign a department when he was hated by his staff and distrusted by many in the criminal-justice system. Sargent kept him on as long as he could, but the pressure kept mounting and Miller didn't help by being the loudmouth he was. Maybe Miller was needed to enact the reform, but somebody else was probably needed to do the mopping up, to make the reform stick.

After Miller's leave-taking, the next commissioner was faced with the task of imposing better control of the contracted programs, negotiating relationships with angry staff, and responding to the problem of proper care for the most difficult, dangerous, and troubled youth. In the face of bureaucratic problems, however, it is important not to lose sight of how at least some young people experienced the shift. One woman told us:

I was being abused by my stepfather and kept running away and getting into trouble. Back when I was first running away, they locked me up with a bunch of tough girls. I was almost as afraid there as I was at home. The last time I ran away [a few years later] they put me in a small girls' school, run by the Episcopal Church, and they treated me like I was somebody who needed help, not like I had done something wrong.

It made me feel a lot better and I stayed there to get my high school education.

Advocacy vs. services for children and elderly

The Department of Elder Affairs and the Office for Children began operations within one year of each other (DEA in November 1971 and OFC in November 1972). Each faced important struggles to establish an identity and a turf for itself. Each was under the leadership of a dynamic head—Jack Leff for DEA and David Leiderman for OFC. Each had an explicit constituency and a commitment to advocacy, making both somewhat new types of public agencies, compared to the older programs that still adopted a more professional, distanced stance toward their clients. Yet, during the Sargent administration, each began to develop very different models for the proper balance between service and advocacy and for the best way to survive in the Massachusetts bureaucratic milieu.[21]

Bureaucratically, the Department of Elder Affairs was a successor to the Elder Affairs Office within the Department of Community Affairs. The old office had also been, as was its replacement, the agency designated to channel federal money from the Older Americans Act (OAA) into the Commonwealth. The agency was also strongly beholden to powerful elderly lobby groups, who were looking for leadership and support from "their" new agency.

At first Leff and his planners sought to incorporate all programs relevant to the elderly, including even Medicaid. They were foiled in this effort by the secretary of Human Services and the others who were unwilling to transfer complex programs to the new agency. DEA then concentrated its efforts on developing and monitoring the Home Care Corporations which provide home-maker and chore services, among other things, to many elderly citizens. This involved the agency in some tense and difficult negotiations with Welfare over purchase of service agreements. The agency developed most of its central staff capacity to oversee these programs and to assist with the allocation of federal OAA money to local Councils on Aging and other programs. It played an advocacy and lobbying role with the legislature and sometimes other agencies, but this was not a primary task under Leff. Indeed, some in the advocacy community were disappointed in the lack of militance of the new department—although they admitted to its important work in establishing itself as the "central broker" in services for the elderly. One legal advocate for the elderly com-mented:

Many people had expected and wanted a "man on a white horse" to fight for the elderly in all arenas. We didn't get that and it was a disappoint-ment. The agency was pretty responsible, however, in what it did do and after a while those of us concerned with elderly advocacy came to realize that DEA was our service, planning, and coordination agency and that we would have to fight for ourselves.

The OFC never had the solid secretariat status that bolstered DEA. Nor was there special federal money or children's issues comparable to OAA. So, during its two years under Sargent, the OFC maintained its identity as an advocacy and coordinating agency that had been the hope of many of its original backers. Children's Councils were set up in local areas to analyze providers and advise on day care contracts and to assume an ombudsman role for parents looking for help for their children. The OFC be-came the licensing agent for day care and had control over some federal seed money to help establish model children's programs which would be transferred later to other agencies.

The Office for Children received its early reputation, however, as an agency that monitored and exposed inadequacies in the children's programs of other agencies, most notably Welfare and Mental Health. Led by David Leiderman, young idealistic "advo-cates for children" became known throughout the system, with varying repercussions. As Brandeis scholar Sandra Frawley ana-lyzed the situation, there were three reactions to the onslaught of OFC "watch puppies": some saw the agency as making people more aware of the need for accountability; others saw it as allowing child advocates within agencies to push more effectively for their goals, as a way to prevent the possibility of OFC criticism; and a few were hostile and critical of the "interference." [22]

Whatever the failures in achieving all its goals, however, the OFC was a recognized entity by the end of 1974. With a staff of committed "change agents" (most of them were paid on consultant contracts because of the difficulty in gaining regular civil service line positions) the OFC and its Children's Councils offered a new role in state agencies. With the advent of Chapter 766 in 1974 (the state law that required local school systems to provide for local children with special needs) this advocacy stance would take on additional community, as well as state, targets.

Regaining Control: 1974–1978

Programs changed dramatically during the Sargent years. New agencies were created and old ones abandoned. The watchword was "innovation." Costs as well as hopes expanded in many areas of human services (see Appendix C).

During Michael Dukakis's administration, which began in 1975, there were fewer dramatic events and more tedious studies calling for better management and fiscal accountability. The style was not to attack services themselves as wasteful or harmful to the family (as would be claimed four years later). It was, instead, to talk about balancing "the real needs for service" with "hard fiscal realities." Expansion had to cease (it already had, in fact, with the FY75 budget, passed in 1974) and reasonable cuts had to be made. In short, the Dukakis administration was characterized—in all areas—by a less impassioned, cooler approach toward services, and a greater emphasis on management techniques for controlling the system.

No one exemplified this approach more than Jerald Stevens, first commissioner of Welfare and then (in January 1976) secretary of Human Services. A systematic, businesslike administrator who knew how to use his intellectual power with a cool, depersonalized arrogance, Stevens worked to down play the crises that had characterized human services development under Sargent and under Lucy Benson (his brief predecessor at EOHS). He developed a set of complex but efficient networks for controlling service expenditures and programs.[23] Stevens kept a small central staff in EOHS and attempted to set up interdepartmental "policy groups" that would oversee planning, evaluation, and budgetary activities. He and many of his key advisers and commissioners were serious, nonprovocative types who failed to evoke either the loyalty or the enmity of many Sargent/Goldmark appointees. All these factors make the story of the years between 1974 and 1978 less colorful. The numbers, charts, and statistics seem as revealing as the narrative. And that legacy would probably please Jerald Stevens.

Managing the Welfare Department:
The Stevens/Sharp administration
A senior manager in the Welfare Department summarized many comments in the differences in DPW brought about by the new administration:

Under Minter, the department talked about greater efficiency and better management. Some better organization was achieved. But few really hard choices were made. The continued need to break down local isolation and to build one united department meant that the administration refused to offend anybody too much. People were always apologizing. Even as recipient militancy declined, the administration was still slow to pull back from mismanaged programs.

The Dukakis people seemed adamant not to make these mistakes. They kept talking about "hard choices," a "management approach," and the need to be "tough." Even when cutbacks were forced by Dukakis, you got the feeling that the top guys really liked making the cuts, that it proved somehow that they were *real* managers.

Shortly after taking office, Governor Dukakis announced that the state faced a serious fiscal crisis that had to be resolved by freezes on state hiring and major spending cuts. For the Welfare Department, these demands were implemented by categorical cuts in Medicaid benefits and the abolition of General Relief (except for disabled individuals unable to work) and special-needs benefits. Such actions were resisted by recipient and advocacy groups but were enacted anyway.[24] A great deal of animosity was created within and outside the department which seemed to set the tone for much of the Stevens/Sharp years. One professional advocate recalled the situation:

Everybody was mad and frustrated. As outside advocates, we felt that Stevens didn't even listen to us about the senselessness of the cuts. Recipient groups got angry and stayed angry and untrusting—although weak— for the whole administration. Inside the department many resented being pushed back into the worst "bad guy" role of the sixties. What especially irked people was that many at the top, especially Stevens, didn't even seem to care about the effects of the cuts or to acknowledge that they imposed hardship.

People acknowledged that he was smart, but a lot of people were resentful and critical for a long time.

Tensions continued even as many of the cuts were restored—a result of advocates' pressure and the lack of feasibility of many of the proposed changes. Intermittent public expressions of concern about fraud and the error rate maintained the climate of resentment among clients and workers. Efforts were made to redesign the work at local offices, to compartmentalize many functions and to take their own case loads away from payments workers—and substitute a more systematic, less personalized system. All of this led to a continuous series of union grievances and court challenges by advocates. The spirit of this time is recaptured in Michael Greenblatt and Steven Richmond's book *Public Welfare: Notes from Underground:*

> In all of this confused and frustrating time [1976] the Department lent no supports to its workers, nor did administrators appear to care about the psychological damage being done to their staff members. The workers themselves thought of quitting, and most considered themselves as being treated like lackeys by the Department. They had been hired as professionals, yet many of them expressed the thought, "they treat us the way they treat clients." [25]

A state workers' strike in the summer of 1976 divided the department. In addition, hiring freezes, and the increasing use of CETA workers, further undermined morale. The governor helped to create a punitive atmosphere by proposing a workfare program that would have forced many recipients to do public work for their welfare checks. Workfare was opposed by Stevens and Sharp as unworkable and inefficent. Professional and recipient advocates mobilized against it. The governor, however, was insistent—even after federal officials were brought in to question the idea. He was finally placated with a small limited program that was given little Departmental support. Workfare, then, plus increased pressures to get women into WIN jobs and to root out fraud, all helped create a widespread sense that the department was increasingly hostile to recipients. One union official recalls that, during the early Dukakis years, "many workers began to complain about feeling like parole officers. They felt under attack themselves but they also felt more pressure to harass clients. Many who had come in the late sixties quit; others sought leave for graduate school. There was a bad feeling everywhere."

Some argue that the last two years of the administration were better, however. The animosity seemed to die down, or, in the words of one worker, "People got numb. Many left and those who stayed began to accept the new reality." Alexander Sharp, the Welfare commissioner, did not project quite the austere, unfeeling image of Stevens, so the department began to "settle down," as one administrator put it.

A contributing factor to the (slowly) evolving better image of the department was the flurry of social services activity that took place after 1975. The new federal social service amendments (Title XX of the Social Security Act) took effect. Among other changes, Title XX forced the state to conduct a more formal and more public planning process, which inevitably involved it with agencies and community groups in a new way. Although Title XX provided no additional money, it offered the option of providing services to more people through the use of sliding fee scales—as long as a "maintenance of effort" was kept for the poor. Another mandate of the Title XX regulations forced the department to create clear contracts with agencies from whom services were purchased, replacing the more open-ended system where vendors were approved and then reimbursed for allowable costs without strict contracts. This system created problems for small vendors and forced the department to take a more legalistic stance toward provider agencies. However, it also began to bring the amount of purchased services to the attention of administrators, other agencies, and the public.

All of these developments made Welfare social services seem far more important than at any time previously. The planning process, especially, made many more people aware of the range of services theoretically available through DPW. For some, the department became, for the first time, a place to consider for "service," not just for money, Medicaid, or relief in cases of child abuse. As one community advocate recalled:

It's not that the department got better. It was more like we began to deal with them about more things, recreation, camps, day care, etc., which had always been there before but somehow we hadn't paid so much attention. The department was still bureaucratic and we didn't get the services we wanted, but somehow the *energy* was different when you were discussing camps for kids than when you were discussing food stamps.

In the Executive Office for Human Services, Stevens created a Social Services Policy Group, composed of leaders from the major agencies, which attempted to consider cross-agency social service policy and to exert coordinated leadership in certain areas. One of

the concerns was over the need to develop expanded training programs for social service workers. Title XX allowed federal matching money to train all direct service workers who were funded by
Title XX, either through contracted programs or as public agency
employees. Within the Welfare Department, the "designated
agency" for administering Title XX, supervisors and some administrators could also be trained.

Title XX training money thus became a new resource which
many saw as a way to improve service delivery and provide better
communication among service agencies, as well as one of the few
new benefits available to service workers.[26] In 1976, 1977, and
1978, a great amount of time was spent by high- and low-level administrators trying to plan and develop a comprehensive training
program for service workers. Area colleges and universities became
involved, as did contracted agency representatives. In 1978—in
what one participant labeled a "tempest in a teapot"—the federal
authorities began questioning the state's plans. By late 1978 substantial money was being spent for training but the political atmosphere surrounding the training expenditures had resulted in
much disillusionment, as described by one welfare official:

After three years of fighting, bureaucratic maneuvering, and "needs as-
sessments" we had disillusioned a lot of people. Many blamed Welfare's
narrow vision. Some people thought that the educational institutions were
too greedy and disunified. Others thought that interagency lack of cor-
respondence was to blame. Even though training finally started, many
people came away thinking that the state couldn't ever do anything right.

During 1977 and 1978, the pressures on DPW service programs
came to a head. Some especially gruesome cases of child abuse and
child death were brought to public attention. Two widely publi-
cized cases involved untrained DPW workers who had been unable to predict the seriousness of abusive situations. Department
representatives reacted with a typical lack of defensiveness. Agency
spokesmen admitted to the problems—and then proceeded to
blame the lack of training, inadequate staffing, and increasing social stress. The department proposed new hot lines and a "review
of staffing patterns," but the overriding image offered to the public
was one of impotence and frustration. One child advocate expressed the implications of the DPW response: "It seemed almost
like they were giving up. They tried to blame the workers, but that
still amounted to an indictment of the department. These were
horrible situations—a dead child chopped up in a garbage bag—
and the department just seemed unable to care or to cope."

Such inadequacy appeared to call for drastic response, and forced many legislators and professionals to return to the call for a separate service agency which had originally been voiced in the 1965 National Study Service Report. In February 1977, a University of Massachusetts study, *The Children's Puzzle,* had also recommended that a separate service agency be established for children and their families. This study had generated some professional and bureaucratic support, but its suggestions had been given little chance of passage until the new exposés of child abuse.

With the public outcry that accompanied these cases, advocates for children, social work professionals, mental health officials, and even some welfare executives began to support the idea of a new agency. The plan was to create a "professional" agency that would focus on children and their families and achieve full separation from the financial and medical concerns of the Welfare Department. In July 1978, much to the surprise of many unfamiliar with such quick government action, the legislature created a new Department of Social Services to take over all service functions from DPW. The mandate of the new agency was broad, as the legislation showed: it was to

formulate the policies, procedures and rules necessary for the full and efficient implementation of programs authorized by the laws of the Commonwealth and federal laws in the area of Social Services; provide those services on a fair, just and equitable basis to all people in need of such services; collaborate with other departments of the Commonwealth which are in fields related to social welfare and with no voluntary or private organizations, to assure efficient and high quality health, mental health, social, educational, correctional and employment services for persons who are unable for social or economic reasons to provide such services for themselves; study the social and economic problems and welfare services in the Commonwealth; and make recommendations to the appropriate branches and agencies of government for broadening and improving the scope and quality of social services. [27]

For all the rhetoric, however, the new agency did not, as some had hoped, take over service functions of other agencies—or lead to any full reorganization of children's services. Instead, the new agency was, fundamentally, only a splitting of the service programs (protective service, adoption, foster care, Title XX, and CHINS) from the Welfare Department, with very little further reorganization.

There were varying responses to the creation of DSS. Some were opposed:

I think it's another runaround. There isn't new money, so the new depart-ment will not provide more services. All we will get will be new adminis-trators. Clients will be more confused about where to go. And it will just be another rat race for workers. [Union official]

Some were skeptical:

All I remember, I think, is that I would have to pay another subway fare to another office to get my day care approved. From our perspective, the new agency never offered anything new, except new rules, new layers of paperwork, and new busy bodies accusing us of child abuse because we can't sweet talk our kids out of being hungry. [Welfare recipient and ad-vocate]

Many of us never thought it would happen. The department said they supported it—under pressure from Stevens—but always seemed lukewarm. Advocates and people from other agencies were divided over how to organize it and who should be in it. It was only all the child-abuse horror stories which finally pushed the legislators to support it as an attempt at "response" to the media barrage. We still don't know if what we got will be better. [Child advocate]

Others were more supportive:

We supported the measure because we felt services deserve more attention than they can get in this department. We also supported it because we want to put all the department's agencies into improving the scope and effi-ciency of AFDC and Medicaid programs—programs which affect more people and use far more resources than social service programs. [Welfare planner]

And others still more supportive:

When the state took over welfare programs, services were just something we provided to poor people because they were in special trouble. We never saw them as programs in themselves, with their own purposes and objec-tives. Over the years services have become that, less of something you just give because a client is in trouble, and more a "right" which people want. We have all sorts of people wanting Title XX services who would never have thought of going to Welfare for services before. Now that the program can be seen this way it really should be separate from AFDC, so that a whole agency can plan and devote its energy to them. [Senior wel-fare official]

Still others see the new agency as representing interagency power struggles:

Mental Health people could get no satisfaction from Welfare. So when the chance came to get a new agency they took it and pushed hard. DSS is really the product of a large campaign by DMH leadership to prove that the Welfare Department is incompetent. [Human service advocate]

The true effect of the new agency would be measured after 1978 but one perspective is inevitable. In many ways the creation of the new department was the final stage of the state takeover of welfare. The arguments for it and its proposed activities could almost have been directly extracted from the 1965 National Study Service report. Administratively, DSS is the logical culmination of the organizational reform begun in 1968.

Leadership and deinstitutionalization
from mental health

The Dukakis administration brought a new commissioner to DMH, Robert Okin. He was young and attractive, a forceful advocate of emptying the state institutions. His previous experience in Vermont had convinced him that a system of "community care" for the retarded and mentally ill was a possible and preferable alternative for almost all residents of state facilities.

Under his leadership, the department began serious, full-scale deinstitutionalization. This meant further development of community mental health centers, expansion of contracted community residences, as well as use of nursing homes and smaller facilities on the grounds of state hospitals. As one mental health worker summarized the thrust:

It was serious. Before, everyone talked about deinstitutionalization, but it was still slow. With Okin that was the one goal. Everyone knew it and it began to happen. No matter what the unions might do or how some might complain about the existence of "alternative care," it was going to happen. Everybody knew it.

In order to accomplish its goals, DMH had to increase its use of contracted services and to push area mental health centers to expand their out-patient and day-treatment facilities. The department had to work closely with DPW to coordinate Title XX and Medicaid funding. It had to present an activist, community-oriented image.

Despite oftentimes hostile local opposition to community residences, and intermittent charges that patients were being "dumped" in communities with no provision for them, a generally positive climate was created. Public relations brochures were produced. Training films were made. The local media systematically covered mental health issues. Indeed, both the expenditure figures and the media image support the contention of one human service advocate:

Mental Health was the leader in everything. Whenever there were efforts at local coordination, Mental Health was there. Whenever there were forums on community services, there they were again. People from Welfare and Rehabilitation, especially, resented this. They felt that Mental Health wanted to be the "innovative leader" while making everybody else take care of their clients. But there is no doubt about it. In spite of the arrogance, when you needed agency support for a new program, you went first to DMH.

Coordinating programs for children and youth

By 1978, both the Office for Children and the Department of Youth Services had settled into more established activities and practices. Although both were still viewed from outside as "more creative and exciting than other, bigger, agencies," internally, workers and administrators saw a standardization of expectations and goals. One DYS worker expressed the mood of interviewees from both agencies:

In some ways things were better. We began to know what we were doing and to have some standard procedures rather than doing everything new. On the other hand, it's not really as much fun, somehow. Somebody called me a "state bureaucrat" the other day and I was insulted.

I used to think of myself as a youth worker who was "fighting the system from within." Maybe it was true that I was always a state bureaucrat but I never felt like one before. Now I'm beginning to.

The Office for Children did maintain its advocacy orientation, however. Under Joyce Strom the agency continued to needle and push local schools and other state agencies—especially DPW. However, the agency became involved in services also. It employed community advocates and representatives who were often placed in local community agencies. These workers were generally still paid as "consultants" or partially covered by funds from the agencies in which they were placed. Much of their work involved advocacy for individuals, referral, and coordination around individual cases. The state office staff provided day care licensing, despite understaffing, and chaired an interdepartmental team which made decisions when no single agency or school was responsible for a particular child.

In short, OFC was active in a range of areas from service to advocacy. The evaluation of The Children's Puzzle writers was that "There is little doubt that OFC has dramatically increased the public consciousness of the needs of children—more people are receiving more service today because of their efforts in the last five years." However, the report also noted several problems with the agency which were echoed by our interviewees: (1) the conflict between the roles of advocacy and coordination, and its effect on state agency relationships; (2) the lack of autonomy needed for advocacy; and (3) the lack of clarity regarding the extent to which services should be delivered by the agency at the local level.[28]

While its activities won OFC many friends among community advocates, it was still an agency without a clear basis of bureaucratic support by 1978. Officials from other agencies were heard to grumble that OFC had "fulfilled its purpose and should be dismantled." Managers wondered whether direct services to children could not be increased if OFC administrative costs were eliminated. The authors of *The Children's Puzzle* did not have to look far to find support for their proposal that the Office for Children be abolished and most of its functions (except licensing and direct advocacy) be transferred to a new state social service agency.

DYS was also slated for abolition by *The Children's Puzzle*, but for different reasons. Since 1974 the department had been continuing to "mop up" after deinstitutionalization and to develop a regional structure of contracted service delivery. DYS continued to provide some services itself but primarily it relied upon contracted services, many of which were new agencies created specifically to meet the need for facilities for DYS youth. To many, new programs seemed uncoordinated and unplanned.

Media attention continued to focus on DYS. Demands continued for more secure facilities and there were still exposés when a child assigned to DYS got into trouble. *The Children's Puzzle* and people interviewed here noted that the department had serious problems monitoring all its contracted services and maintaining quality in state facilities.[29] One DYS official might feel pride:

Sometimes we forget that it's only been ten years since the department was founded. Ten years since all delinquent kids were in state schools, wearing uniforms and having their heads shaved. We may still be the smallest department and still have a lot of difficulty defining our "mission," but we've really made a big difference in a short time.

At the same time, another state official, from DMH, could express a different, widely held opinion:

They still don't know whether to be a juvenile corrections agency or a service agency. Their kids are in trouble with the law and some are pretty tough. A lot of people outside the agency, and more than will admit it inside, think the priority should be on corrections. The push has been toward services and intervention but that takes a lot of time, skill, and money for kids as difficult as theirs. And they don't have any of those commodities in abundance.

Relative success for the elderly

By 1978, one naturally critical human service advocate could say:

The Department of Elder Affairs is O.K. I mean, organizationally they're crazy because of the federal funding and the Home Care Corporations, but the people are good. You get the sense that it's staffed by a bunch of competent, caring people who admit to a struggle with hard problems. We hear lots of complaints about Area Agencies for the Elderly and about Home Care services. When we talk to people at DEA they are willing to admit to the problems in a way which is unlike the defensiveness of other agencies.

It seems strange for me to say this but somehow I think it's because of how people feel about the elderly. Nobody hates the elderly or blames them for their needs. So the agency isn't under too much attack.

This sentiment was shared by others, who also attributed the good feeling to such factors as limited scope, good leadership, and a strong constituency.

The first Dukakis appointee as commissioner, Rose Claffey, was replaced in 1977 by Jim Callahan. During Claffey's term old issues of service vs. advocacy and the appropriate relationships with DPW re-emerged. During this period it was often lumped with OFC as "an agency searching for an identity." Under the calm and stable Callahan tenure, however, the older pattern of 1973–74 was re-established. The agency played a limited advocacy role and settled for a coordinative and generally supportive relationship with local and federally funded programs. Continuing negotiations were carried on with DPW around Medicaid and Title XX funding. Relationships were built with Social Security and Massachusetts Rehabilitation regarding SSI eligibility determinations. In short, by 1978, DEA was the agency to come through the reorganization battles of the 1970s with a generally favorable reputation and a sense of "mission accomplished."

Continued reform: the quest for an area strategy

As we have seen, a major structural problem in Massachusetts human services from 1966 until 1978 was the tension between whether to centralize or decentralize service delivery. As one senior welfare official put it:

The task of the late sixties/early seventies for DPW was to centralize, to get more control and accountability. After accomplishing this, our next task was to decentralize again, to put the appropriate authority back at the delivery level. It may look like going back, but it is not. We are decentralizing in different ways than we did before, in a planned, not armchair, way.

Most state agencies experienced similar difficulties. The twin themes of "community care" and "efficient management" often exerted contradictory pressures. State agencies were pushed from above to become more accountable, to develop more standardized procedures for disbursement of funds and delivery of services. Yet each was also urged (through the media, by client groups, advocates, and unions) to be more responsible to local needs and more flexible and less bureaucratic. Indeed, most agencies needed to improve in both areas. But the simultaneous development of both capacities usually proved institutionally impossible.

Instead there were pendular swings in each direction. Sometimes there would be stress on efficiency and accountability. Other times the pressure would shift to an emphasis on local delivery and organization. To increase the confusion, at different times different agencies were at different stages of the process. For instance, DYS was decentralizing while DPW was centralizing. More recently, in 1978, the Office for Children began efforts to strengthen its central staff, just as other agencies were beginning to copy its earlier model of local emphasis.

In 1977, Jerald Stevens began to support one of the few programmatic efforts directly undertaken by EOHS, the Area Strategy project. Area Strategy was an outgrowth of a service integration experiment begun in 1973 in the Taunton area.[30] In Taunton, the plan to deinstitutionalize the state hospital had been accompanied by an effort to involve other community agencies and private resources in the joint planning for services for ex-patients and people with newly identified needs. Led by a forceful area director of Mental Health, the Taunton project attracted local and national attention. Federal grant money was procured and the "Taunton model" was seized upon by Stevens and others as a way to harmonize the centralization-decentralization pressures for all agencies.

With the support of Stevens, the Social Services Policy Committee and federal grant money, Area Strategy was launched as the major thrust for Massachusetts state social service delivery. Hearings were held in local areas to determine service priorities and to determine the locale of demonstration projects which were to precede the full adoption of area strategy. Area agencies were pressured to meet together and plan joint activities. As demonstration projects were funded—also using some special Title XX funds —they tried to develop different models for bottom-up human service administration. Central offices were still needed to set overall policy and monitor funding and program standards, but decentralization to the area level was to be an overall goal.

Area Strategy generated much heat during its brief life. Its brash, creative, and difficult director, Robert Curtis, was always offending someone. Many state central-office officials were skeptical of an EOHS-initiated effort to decentralize their programs, especially because the roots of the approach went back to Mental Health. On the other hand, local area staff and advocates were skeptical of "another innovation" and also doubtful that there would ever be real autonomy.

Finally, the project fell of its own weight. Internal divisions developed between EOHS officials and Area Strategy staff over the degree of autonomy that local Area Strategy teams (made up of local officials and private providers) would exercise. When Stevens announced his resignation in August 1978 the end was near. Some newspaper reports detailed "improprieties" in the fiscal relationship between Area Strategy projects and the state. The director was forced to resign and monies were frozen. Although the demonstration projects went on in selected local areas, the state's commitment to a unified approach to decentralized service delivery was disbanded.

Closure

Later chapters will analyze the results of our still schematic history. Here we can only be aware of how little we have covered, how much more could be said about each program, about each period. What is most striking, however, is consistent development, from 1966 onward, of the slow but constant growth of a self-contained, acknowledged, and interdepartmental system of human services. This system, although troubled and plagued by self-hatred as well as external hostility, was at its core increasingly linked to the Department of Public Welfare. Despite its ideological and policy leadership, the Department of Mental Health became increasingly involved with welfare recipients and welfare funding. As they left state hospitals and schools, many patients became recipients of SSI or General Relief. The "community programs" that served them were often dependent on Medicaid or Title XX monies from Welfare.

Elderly and children's services became similarly dependent on

Chart 3   Time Line of Selected Events in the Development of
Massachusetts Human Services 1966–1978 *

	Feds	DPW	DMH
Pre-1966	1935–Social Security Act 1963–Community Mental Health Centers Act 1965–Medicaid 1965–Older Americans Act	1956–DCG formed 1963–Robert Ott, commissioner 1965 (Dec.)–National Study Service, *Report*	1965–*Mental Health in Massachusetts* calls for community care
1966 to 1970	1967–Social Service Amendments/WIN 1968–Richard Nixon, president 1969–Requirements for separation of payments and services	1966–Medicaid begins 1968 (July)–State takeover 1968–Great increase in welfare costs	1966–Chapter 735 mandates reorganization 1967–Milton Greenblatt, commissioner 1968–First halfway house for the retarded
1970 to 1974	1972–Federal cap on social service expenditures 1972–Talmadge Amendments strengthen WIN	1970–Steven Minter, commissioner 1970–Flat Grant 1971–Purchase of service begins 1972–WIN expands 1973–CHINS to DPW	1970–Mental Health Reform Act limits hospital commitments 1971–Lawsuits demand better care 1971–Talks with DPW for Medicaid $ for deinstitutionalization 1973–Robert Goldman, commissioner
1974 thru 1978	1974 (Jan.)–SSI begins 1974–Gerald Ford, president 1975–Title XX 1976–Jimmy Carter, president	1974–Food stamps begin statewide 1974–Services and payments separated 1975–Jerald Stevens, commissioner 1975–Cuts in GR, Medicaid, EA 1976–Alexander Sharp, commissioner 1976–Title XX initiated 1978–Child abuse scandals 1978–DSS mandated	1975–Robert Okin, commissioner 1975–Deinstitutionalization becomes dominant priority
Post-1978	1980–Ronald Reagan, president 1981–Budget cuts and block grant strategy	1980–DSS begins 1981–Workfare proposed	1981–Slowdown of deinstitutionalization; Blue Ribbon Commission, *Report*

* For meaning of acronyms, see Appendix G

Other programs	Clients	State climate
	1964–Parents of retarded children organize 1965–MAWS organize in Boston	1965–Poverty Programs begin
1966–HEW report is critical of Youth Services 1968–Plans passed for state reorganization 1969–DYS formed, Jerry Miller, commissioner	1967–MWRO organizes 1968–Welfare militancy increases 1969–Children's and elder advocates organize	1966–Volpe/Sargent, governors 1967–Riots in Roxbury 1968–Riots in Roxbury 1969–Francis Sargent, governor
1971–New cabinet system begins: Peter Goldmark, EOHS secretary 1971–DEA begins, Jack Leff, secretary 1972–DYS empties institutions 1972–OFC begins, David Leiderman, director 1973–Jerry Miller leaves DYS 1973–Chapter 766 enacted 1973–Rate-setting commission established	1972–*Suffer the Children* criticizes children's services 1972–Welfare activism fades	1973–State economy declines
1975–Lucy Benson, EOHS secretary 1975–Alliance of public sector unions 1976–Jerald Stevens, EOHS secretary 1976–Mass. Council of Human Service Providers formed 1976–State workers strike 1977–*Children's Puzzle* calls for reorganization of services 1977 thru 1978–Area Strategy	1975–Professional/client alliance to fight cuts	1974–Michael Dukakis, governor
1981–EOHS proposes reorganization	1979–Coalition for Basic Human Needs forms 1979–Children's advocates fight for OFC	1978–Edward King, governor 1980–Proposition 2½ passes 1981–Budget cuts begin

Welfare. DPW had stable, open-ended funding for the income and medical support of clients as well as the largest pool of general service dollars. Therefore, during the period under inquiry, planners and administrators, consumers, workers, and advocates increasingly looked to Welfare and its programs for poor people as the most reliable funding base for specialized program development.

The pressures of being the hub of this emerging human service system were not easily borne by a Welfare Department created in 1968, staffed by civil servants with varied training and saddled with great fiscal and public pressures. The department frequently exhibited an institutional "digging in of the heels" and was often perceived by others as reactionary, overly bureaucratic, or inept. Yet the expectations of the department were indeed great, as expressed by one career welfare staff person:

Sure, we often looked bad. But you have to remember that we are the only agency that can't say "no." Mental Health, they can just dump somebody out of the hospital. Children grow up. Other agencies find some loophole. We had to deal with everybody and be responsible for everything, and all the time with the worst offices, the lowest status, and the worst publicity. Sure, the other agencies said they wanted innovation and cooperation. But all they wanted was Welfare Department money so they could run their programs and get the credit.

The remainder of this study will analyze and criticize the patterns, pressure points, and dynamics of this emerging system—a system with a reluctant Welfare Department at its center, and many dependent, yet highly autonomous, sister agencies on its edges.

4 Special Effects

There are many dimensions to the Circle Game. Knowing the chronology of events and re-creating a narrative of how they occured is helpful, and sets the stage for more specialized analyses. But there were also on-going and shifting processes which affected how human services developed during this period, that do not fit neatly into a time line. To understand the complexity of influences we must break away from the historical account and examine the special effects created by such factors as federal priorities and initiatives; the peculiar pressures of the Massachusetts environment; the roles of the courts, the legislature, and the media; and the human interactions within the system. This chapter, then, is an attempt to consider the impact of such processes from 1966 to 1978 and to establish a background for speculating on how the Circle Game will be played in the future.

The National Background

Since the passing of the Social Security Act in 1935 it has been impossible to consider state social welfare programs without awareness of national initiatives and mandates.[1]

Throughout the period under review, Washington provided both the money and the guidelines under which Massachusetts developed and administered social programs. As we have seen, the federal presence was felt in many different areas of the Massachusetts human service system. Initially, there was the provocative presence of federally funded poverty programs which helped low-income communities raise issues and highlight problems that had been effectively buried earlier. The Community Mental Health Centers Act in 1963 also provided resources and ideological support for those wishing to develop community-based services. The importance of the 1965 passage of Title XIX of the Social Security Act, Medicaid, was felt across the Commonwealth by 1966, and was increasingly responsible for substantial growth in costs. The passage of Title XX, the social service amendment, meant new rules and new programs after 1975. The Older Americans Act (1965) and changes in national conceptions of juvenile justice also fostered evolving patterns of service delivery.

Such legislation created new options and, even though new money was less available by the mid 1970s, it still fostered a climate of federal support for growth or redesign, rather than an atmosphere of cutbacks and retrenchment. Furthermore, most of the new legislation, even under the Nixon administration, resulted from pressure by professional leaders who were either from Massachusetts or were in close association with public and private sector professionals from the Commonwealth.

As important as new legislation was changing national leadership. From Johnson to Nixon to Ford to Carter, the federal perspective shifted in regard to social programs. Under Johnson, the federal interest and energy was focused on large-scale program developments which appeared to tackle social problems in a robust way. Under Nixon and Ford, the thrust was managerial: states were pressured to be more "efficient," to reorganize in order to avoid duplication and wasted efforts. With Carter's administration the emphasis swung to a stress on support for individualized care for the most needy, rather than a broad-brush attack on generalized social problems. Although somewhat subtle, these varying federal pressures, expressed in speeches, research, and development options, as well as program regulations, were as influential as congressional mandates in effecting the tone and style of Massachusetts human service programs.[2]

While it is not our purpose here to review in detail all these national programmatic and procedural developments, a few points must be made in order to understand the Massachusetts programs during the period under review.

First, Massachusetts experienced the same federal pressures as did other states and developed similar patterns of growth. For instance, national studies of poverty programs indicate that everywhere in the country such programs created new pressures on state and local bureaucracies; they established new models of advocacy around service issues and provided new examples of how services could be deprofessionalized and decentralized.[3] And in many cities across Massachusetts, local community action agencies trained a new breed of young service activists who put pressure on the state agencies for more accountable procedures and more "community-based" programs.

The growth of community mental health centers and deinstitutionalization were similar in Massachusetts to patterns in other states. Medicaid costs soared here as they did elsewhere, although the great availability of high-technology medicine and the variety of medical expertise in the state possibly led to greater increases here than in many other states. And the seventies' patterns of bureaucratic restructuring and increased use of purchased services were found in most other states as well as in Massachusetts.[4]

In short, it is important to acknowledge that when Massachusetts officials joined with other states in reacting to federal human service mandates, they did not stand alone. At professional meetings and federal briefings Massachusetts delegates usually responded to federal proposals in patterns common to other industrialized, urbanized states like New York, Illinois, Pennsylvania, and California. For all the specialness of particular circumstances, we cannot forget that in most ways federal officials often viewed Massachusetts as just another big state, albeit one with many influential professionals, which wanted its way.[5]

Second, federal dollars were a critical support to the Massachusetts human service system during this period. AFDC and Medicaid costs were covered by at least 50 percent federal reimbursement, and social service costs by a 75 percent rate (although as service costs expanded, a federal ceiling effectively cut federal participation). SSI had almost total federal support. Deinstitutionalization, while not a federal program, was highly federally subsidized, as were programs in Elderly Affairs and Massachusetts Rehabilitation.[6] General Relief was the major state program not supported by any federal dollars; and it was noticeably a program that suffered severe cuts. To speak, then, of the Massachusetts human service system during this period is to speak of a set of programs that were substantially supported by federal dollars and where the broad operations and directions were, to a large measure, governed by federal regulations.

Third, federal money meant federal control. The day-to-day operations of most of the programs listed above were defined by federal regulations governing eligibility, implementation options, management procedures, mandated evaluation, and monitoring processes, to name only a few areas. State regulations and guidelines often went beyond federal requirements, but federal procedures formed the base upon which programs were built. However, DPW, DMH, DEA, and Mass. Rehab., especially, had been operating for so long within federal constraints that such regulations were often not considered federal "pressure." Only in relation to changes and new programs were federal initiatives mentioned. Yet it is obvious that all major programs under discussion were most influenced by decisions made in Washington, not Boston—and certainly not in the local community.

Despite the widespread federal involvement, few policy makers referred to national pressures as forcing unwanted program change (except for increased paperwork). Instead, most characterized the relationship with federal authorities as "amiable" and one that could often be used to advantage. One administrator expressed it this way:

The regional feds were usually straightforward with us—after all, they were following well-known Washington policy. When we wanted something which the legislature could not understand, we would let them know that a little federal pressure might be appreciated and then we would blame them for our demands. In many ways we had an extra advantage. Often we could bypass our regional people if we didn't like what they said, then we would go over their heads to Washington.

On a day-to-day basis, then, the federal influence on state program activities was not intense, once regulations and guidelines were followed. National politics often kept federal bureaucrats in as much, or more, turmoil than state officials experienced. Federal changes in personnel and policy were rapid and the morale was frequently low. State officials learned to "watch and wait." While new eager state managers might worry about the feds, old-timers were more relaxed, if not cynical, as one upper-level manager described: "We knew we could handle the feds most of the time. Even though they paid the money they were somewhat afraid of us. We were the 'program people' who knew what could really be done. Sometimes they were forced to pressure us for new procedures or better documentation, but mainly they listened to us and left us alone."

Finally, when federal authorities were influential throughout this period, it was in regard to fiscal and procedural matters, not program content. Changing mandates and new federal priorities were usually experienced in the field as new forms to fill out, new "accountability measures" to be met. Seldom was the service content of programs in question. Even case-load issues or fraud and error-rate concerns were finally reduced to numeric calculations. Federal monitors might visit programs and make nervous administrators anxious, but even critical reports usually lacked serious clout, especially those relating to the operations of the larger public bureaucracies. Where cases were pushed or funding withheld, federal officials did seem to exhibit some power. But most administrators we met discussed these situations as the necessary and standard bureaucratic pressures, not harassment.

We find, then, something of a paradox. During most of this period, shifting federal initiatives expressed in new legislation, programs, and regulations were crucial to the development of human service programs in Massachusetts. Witness the impact of Medicaid, the Community Mental Health Center Act, SSI, the Older Americans Act, Title XX, or the food stamp program. Yet, at the state and local levels, few policy makers, workers, or clients remember being obsessed about federal pressure. Workers often recall that national changes were blamed when working conditions changed: "Whenever we complained about the increased work involved with some new procedure, the answer was that 'we had no choice, the Feds were to blame.' I never knew whether to believe them or not." And client advocates remember fighting proposed federal regulations: "Mainly, I remember fighting Washington when something new was being proposed, like Nixon's planned program, the Talmadge Amendment, or Carter's welfare reforms. Usually we could fight better here." But, in general, we found an amazing lack of concern with national issues among people whose daily lives were, to a large extent, defined by federal regulations.

When officials and/or advocates were in agreement with national mandates, they were adopted, embraced, even publicly used to provide a rationale for desired changes. And, during this period, there did not appear to be great disharmony between federal and state directions. When there was disagreement—such as when federal regulations demanded separation of welfare services and payments—state officials postponed compliance, ignored directives, and generally tried to "wait out" the federal authorities. Sometimes matters ended up in court or in nasty hearings, but more often the strategy seemed to work and achieve a compromise.

Of course, some of this pattern should not be surprising, given the nature of American federalism and of bureaucratic politics.[7] But looking back today, when "federal mandates" mean cuts and when a sizable number of professionals, politicians, and citizens in Massachusetts—if not upper-level administrators—are in disagreement with federal directives, the philosophical harmony exhibited during this period seems hard to believe. Yet it clearly contributed to the operation of the Circle Game in this period, and may be deeper than we want to think, as suggested by one mid-level administrator:

You must not forget that we are all bureaucrats, and most of us accept the rules of the bureaucracy. We know we need to carry out the federal and state rules so we don't think to question them. The people in Washington who make those rules are just like us; unless they want us to do the impossible, we go along and then try to be creative about how.

During the time you are talking about [1966–1978] a lot of people liked the rules from Washington so it seemed OK to you to follow them. But that wasn't why people in Welfare went along, we went along because it was our job and would have gone along with other rules if we had to. Don't fool yourself.

Massachusetts Eccentricities

Massachusetts has many special traditions which affect the delivery of public services. Long-held habits and assumptions have created patterns of expectations that are deep, if often unspoken. Taken together these eccentricities formed another set of rules for the Circle Game, a group of rules that were powerful exactly because they were left unstated.

The first expectation in Massachusetts has long been that legislation and stated policy mandates will be liberal, often the most liberal in the nation. Massachusetts, during the period reviewed here, was a leader in forming policy for mental health, special education, the deinstitutionalization of youth services. The necessary corollary to this expectation, though, is that neither the public nor the politicians seemed to expect full implementation of these grand and beautifully written policies. Indeed, it has often been taken as naiveté if an overzealous administrator did try too hard actually to carry out policy mandates.

To some extent such hypocrisy is the norm with all social policy. Yet few states have enacted so many seemingly generous policies as Massachusetts. Most seem willing to promise less. Perhaps the source of this contradiction goes back to the Puritan roots of Boston, where leaders felt obliged to assert that they had created a "City of a Hill," regardless of the failures of implementation.[8] Most certainly, the historical split between upper-class Brahmin and working-class Irish and other immigrants continued the accepted dichotomy.

Brahmins wrote legislation and planned policy that would continue to prove the ideal that, as Governor Dukakis loved to assert,

Massachusetts was "the Athens of America." They did not, however, appropriate the funds to cover the full enactment of such programs. Brahmins, also, left implementation up to the Irish or other "outside" groups who retained a profound skepticism about the possibility of real generosity from a class known to be so personally withholding and judgmental.

The split was best exemplified by the different attitudes we found between upper-level administrators and those who delivered services: all of the leadership spoke with some hope of "policy mandates" which would create better services and a more humane system. They expressed concern for the client and sympathy with current progressive trends in human services. Often they blamed the civil servants, the unions, and the conservative public for problems in their programs. In contrast, the workers we interviewed often presented themselves as personally more traditional, with both more anger and more fear in regard to clients, new program reforms, and the professionals.

Such attitudes served to institutionalize the distance between liberal policies and restrictive practices. Upper-class politicians and middle-class professionals could unite to pass generous or impossible programs and then blame the workers for program failures. Workers, consistently facing impossible goals and limited resources, understood that they could only fail to implement liberal policies so they became cynical about ever achieving the caring goals of human services.[9] Everybody played according to the rules of the Circle Game and nobody won.

Another tension within Massachusetts human services has been the battle between professionals (in social work, medicine, and public administration) and politicians. There were many jobs in the state, and politicians often wished to fill them. So did the powerful social work and medical schools. The period we examined saw major victories for the professionals. "Upgrading" and training were the watchwords, especially in Welfare and Mental Health. Local and state politicians had less access to the human service jobs than they had prior to Sargent's administration. Indeed, several administrators referred to the creation of the Department of Social Services as the "triumph of the professional approach." The new agency was to improve on old patterns using the ultimate weapon, trained professionals, in place of untrained bureaucrats. While the election of a new governor and the existence of a less professionally influenced administration in Washington may work against an increase in influence for professionals, it is unlikely that these patterns can be totally reversed.

In addition, the importance of professional influence was felt in another aspect of the Massachusetts human service system. The extent to which "private" resources were viewed as superior to public services, throughout the development of human services in Massachusetts, directly reflected the greater role trained professionals played in private agencies, programs, and hospitals. Unlike the Far West and Midwest, where public programs have often been the best programs, in Massachusetts public services and programs have long been viewed as "the last resort," both for professional workers seeking employment and for consumers seeking services. The result is that this bias has become a self-fulfilling phophecy.

Another important aspect of the Massachusetts environment was the power of local cities and towns, and the impact of rivalries among them. In most other states, the county has long been the important unit of service delivery and point of identification —incorporating the different histories and practices of local communities. In Massachusetts, individual cities and towns vie for resources and status, while the counties are insubstantial. Although most state programs are independent of local governments, they still must function within the local milieu, thereby creating conflicting pressures for local workers and clients, who may feel more loyal to their town than their agency. Further, many legislators and administrators often feel little loyalty or concern for the problems of other cities and towns. This problem plagued the Welfare Department, but also influenced the progress of deinstitutionalization and the development of other community-based services. Another aspect of this problem has been the tradition of anti-Boston sentiment throughout the Commonwealth. Because Boston does, indeed, have a higher percentage of people needing services than many other areas, due to its higher poverty levels and urban problems, some of the legislative and public hostility to many human service expenditures was seen by some as reflecting long-standing hostility to Boston.

The location of the legislature in Boston had a mixed effect on human services, as one upper-level administrator recalled:

They were right up the street. We could go to them directly, which was often good, when we needed something. On the other hand, lobbyists of all types, or people without money, could get to them more easily than is possible in places like Albany, Sacramento, or other state capitals. Since the early seventies, they have been more involved with mundane human service problems; their staffs have been poking around a lot.

It might be easier if we were off in some little cow town, away from the day-to-day problems, but then, I'm not sure.

Whatever the final judgment on their role, it has been true that the presence of all state offices and the state legislature in the turmoil of Boston created on-going, special pressures on the system, more extreme than the situations in many other states. When welfare mothers sat in, the handicapped rallied, or children were found abused, the media was there; the governor, the legislature, and agency heads had to act on the spot. At least the close proximity served to heighten any crisis that occurred and brought high-level administrators closer to the daily fray than often happens in other states.

Finally, Massachusetts has been a state where ethnic divisions and political pressures are especially influential. Underlying disputes among Irish and Italians, Wasps and Jews, Blacks and Puerto Ricans emerge in locating halfway houses, in appointments of commissioners and in the definition of "service priorities." While such divisions may only serve to hide deeper divisions between the upper and working classes—or between management and labor—they are often the defining reality for clients and workers in the human services, making them realistically skeptical of "rational" plans for program change:

We all know that being Irish helps in the Welfare Department. Local services still suffer because staff don't come from the same background as their clients. Under Dukakis this improved some, but not much. In general, the best ticket to success in state agencies is to be Irish—or maybe Italian—and to go to Boston College. [Local service worker]

From Back Wards to Fishbowl

Three important areas increasingly influenced the human services during the period under review, and each played an important, if unpredictable, role in the on-going process of the Circle Game. The courts grew in importance, as did the legislature and the media, for some similar and critical reasons.

One senior-level administrator was adamant about the importance that legal issues had come to assume:

You cannot talk about the human service "system" anymore without including the courts and the lawyers. Legal staffs in all the agencies have grown rapidly over the past few years, because we have learned that anything we do may be challenged in court. It all really started with "consent decrees" issued to stop poor treatment in state schools for the retarded. Then other client groups learned to use the courts, as well as our appeals processes, by using legal service attorneys.

I'm not saying it's bad, really. The legal system is there to make us enforce the laws, but it gets crazy when one state agency launches suits against another, as the Office for Children did against Welfare. It used to be that Mental Health dealt with the courts only around commitments, and Welfare only around abuse cases. Now it feels like all we do is go to court about something. It's like all the services have become legal issues.

Other advocates acknowledge that "legal remedies" have become more important, but see the problem somewhat differently, as one community advocate remarked:

Sure, it's become more legalistic. But that's because it's the only weapon people still have, cumbersome as it may be. As times have gotten harder, the agencies have almost become dependent on us to go to court to stop them, or to make them do what they should be doing anyway—like hiring more workers or improving conditions in the institutions.

My worry is that we rely on the lawyers too much. The courts can go against us, too, and we haven't really won, even when a case does go our way. We still have to organize to make sure they do what they have to do, and if we've depended too much on the lawyers we may not be strong enough to do that.

Interesting similarities can be seen when we examine how participants viewed the legislators' role in the definition of programs, especially after 1974. Administrators complain that, although legislators had always been involved in certain key budgeting and organizational crises—like the takeover of welfare or the enactment of Medicaid—their influence increased in unhealthy ways during the period. Again, our senior administrator was insistent:

Now they think everything is their business, not just big changes. Committee aides drive us crazy with requests for information. If we spent all the time required to collect all the data they wanted we wouldn't do anything. They pay us to run programs and, ever since Dukakis came in, they won't leave us alone and let us do it.

And, again, activists see the same pattern but explain it as another natural reaction to bad, mismanaged programs. Asked specifically about the requests for information one advocate replied, "That's just self-serving baloney. They don't want to tell anybody anything. The legislative committees are the only ones able to get anything out of them." One committee especially, the Human Services Committee, was praised by advocates as playing an important role in keeping watch over "efficiency-oriented" managers and a rigid governor. "We need allies wherever we can get them. It's too bad the administration doesn't like the meddling. It's public money, after all."

Still further parallels emerge when we examine feelings expressed about the media. Administrators again express similar fears of increased influence: "Maybe it's my imagination, but I don't think they used to care so much about human services. Now anything can be on local TV or in the newspapers, taken out of context. The treatment of the child abuse cases was just the most extreme example." And advocates see the same mixed opportunities: "We have learned to use the media better over the years. There are more local TV programs especially. But you have to be careful, because reporters can twist things and then arouse the old 'everyone on welfare is a free-loading good-for-nothing' myth."

There is a factual base for all the perceptions expressed. The period studied did witness a great increase in the use of the courts by advocacy groups. Consent decrees were issued to force state institutions to improve in the late 1960s and continued to play a role in mental health policy and programs throughout the seventies. Similar decisions were also used to push the Welfare Department to hire more social workers and to force compliance with other regulations or to stop illegal practices. Many of these suits, but not all, were brought with the assistance of legal service attorneys, who were also actively involved in providing individual legal services to poor people. Certainly, compared to the situation in 1966, the legal field of administrative advocacy in the human services had grown in size and sophistication by 1978.[10]

The legislature, too, increased its involvement in human services. As we have noted, the state takeover of welfare suddenly made welfare costs more evident. After 1972, fiscal pressures in the state budget meant that expensive service programs received greater scrutiny, especially as Medicaid costs and the costs of deinstitutionalization drove budgets up. And, with the Dukakis administration's new emphasis on efficiency, a breed of managers emerged who had a manner quite different from that of older administrators. Their arrogant style quite openly infuriated some old-line politicians. So an old pattern was intensified: advocates (and some shy, dissident bureaucrats) would go directly to legislators who then raised public inquiries. It was not a new model, and it is hard to measure, but many people interviewed mentioned this as an important development over the period under review—especially when the legislators were unhappy with Governor Dukakis.

Similarly, the involvement of the local media in human service concerns did increase. Local programming grew dramatically from 1966 to 1978.[11] As the air time increased so did "human interest" stories which might include clips on deinstitutionalization, day care, youth services, or welfare fraud. Similarly, our impressionistic review of the *Boston Globe* over the period showed a marked increase in stories on social programs from 1966 to 1978, with the greatest change seeming to occur in the early seventies. Newspaper coverage was sporadic; sometimes the writer on the "state-house beat," for instance, seemed to take an interest in one agency, like Mental Health, and then there would be consistent follow-through for a sustained period. At other times only crisis stories would make the papers. But human service "crises" seemed to increase throughout the 1970s, and to attract more media coverage.

In short, the growing legal, legislative, and media activity made people in the world outside of human services more aware of and involved in the system during the time studied. And one involvement led to another. Court cases spawned more court cases. Successful suits led to others as lawyers, recipients of services, and their families became aware of ways to affect the delivery of services from the outside. One legislative hearing, receiving good publicity, seemed to breed another. Similarly, newspaper stories on welfare generated letters and follow-up stories. The increasing involvement of middle-class and upper middle-class professionals with state agencies meant that people with access to the media and a more marketable personal style were leaking stories to the *Globe* and to friendly TV reporters. Advocacy groups learned to use the courts and the media to go around normal channels. Human service decisions moved out of dingy bureaucrats' meetings —and local welfare offices and state institutions—into the more public arena of the media, the State House, and the courts.

The effects of such changes are hard to assess. Optimists would see them as an indication that human services are more integrated into the wider concerns of the community, more publicly identified as a "public good" to be scrutinized, fought over, and defended. Pessimists might wonder whether all the attention tends to "blame the victim," to individualize—either by romanticization or hostility—the problems that social programs address and to set unreasonable organizational standards for a system with few real friends. For now, the point is that both results were probably applicable and helped to make the Circle Game more visible, if still not understandable, to a far wider audience than ever before.

What's Public? What's Private?

Massachusetts has a long history of strong, private philanthropy and private charity. The private social work schools in the state are among the best in the nation. The private social welfare community was instrumental in producing the National Study Service report that called for a state takeover of the local welfare system. Private professionals also led the call for a reorganization of youth services. There can be no doubt that when the social workers in Massachusetts combine their credentials and influence with that of the private psychiatric community, they together form a powerful lobby for whatever they choose to define as "progress."

However, events of the past ten years have radically changed the relationships of this "private sector" to the public human service system. Medicaid funding has provided a major source of "third-party payments" to mental health and health professionals. Title XX contracts have become the main source of funding for many private agencies. And, finally, the availability of Title XX training money brought social work educators flocking to the public trough. The situation is such that a Massachusetts political observer could note:

There are no true independents in human services any more. All the social workers and psychiatrists have an interest in the system, and the legislators are not dumb. They know that the so-called experts in the field depend on the state to fund their agencies—even the cardinal's charities need the state—or to provide training grants to their schools. So the legislators don't trust anybody's advice any more. They just react on instinct. And when the Massachusetts legislature does that, watch out.

Some social workers denied a decrease in influence, and pointed to the continued role of professionals in various advocacy groups. But others were more critical, arguing for the need to be "realistic," like this social worker from a private agency:

"Maybe we aren't so pure any more—there is no denying that. Hell, professionals have to eat too. But we are still the community that knows more about service delivery than anybody else and they [the legislature] would be stupid to forget that."

There are many reasons for this increased spending of public money on private services, a pattern that occurred across the country during this period.[12] Medicare and Medicaid had been sold to the medical profession, at least in part, because of the promise of increased revenues for health institutions and doctors —and the system lived up to its promise. Public spending for private social services increased after 1967 due to public and private officials' desire to improve the amount and quality of services without expanding the increasingly unionized and bulky public bureaucracies. And deinstitutionalization policies in mental health and youth services were based, in part, upon plans to hire more flexible, cheaper, nonpublic workers to staff community residences, not higher paid, more specialized civil servants.

The end result of such changes was a system where the private sector was not public and where the public sector increasingly provided fewer and fewer services while it contracted to "private providers." This situation would, at least, seem to call for a redefinition of roles which did not occur during the period under scrutiny. In 1975 many state provider agencies came together to pressure the Welfare Department into providing standard and realistic contracts. This association grew into the Massachusetts Council of Human Service Providers, which attempted to combine an advocacy role with involvement in state planning activities. In doing this, the council and other provider groups came to be viewed by state officials as another arm of the system. Perhaps the comments of one welfare administrator best sum up the problems of provider/public relationships as they developed throughout this period:

I'm never quite sure how to relate to them. Many of them have better education and more expertise than we do here in the department. Some of them are very well connected to legislators and the schools of social work. Sometimes they come in with all these professional judgments and demands about how we have to do better. But the next day they will be back trying to negotiate a contract which is vague and unclear and which doesn't tell the department enough about what they are going to do for us to monitor them. They expect us to trust them but, in their professional role, they want us to "enforce accountability" on the whole system.

It's hard. I understand how it happens. They really are wearing two hats, but somehow it doesn't work. After all, in many ways they are our employees but they act like our bosses.

The Human Dimension

The institutional overview presented in the last chapter tends to leave out many of the people involved. Client militancy and "frauds" make their way into the story, as do allegations of worker incompetence or error. But the narrative does not reveal ongoing developments within the work force or the recipient groups. In this way, the history reflects a standard omission of policy makers and program designers: the human beings who provide the service (by allocating money or food stamps, for example) or who *are* the service (by listening, talking, or battling the system for clients) are often forgotten or assumed to be infinitely flexible. Similarly, clients are assumed to be eternally passive recipients of services and their preferences and ability to use services are seldom seriously considered.

Many people interviewed noted that the period under review was a "bad time" for human service workers in Massachusetts. We heard comments like:

It was like they kept setting workers against clients. Closing down state hospitals meant threats to our jobs but we weren't supposed to complain because it was better for clients. Extended hours of community service were "more responsive" but we never got more staff so we were strapped. It often felt like all the reforms in DMH had to come out of our hides. [Mental health worker]

We unionized and I guess that was good for us but sometimes I don't know. The one thing we used to have going for us was that we were the professionals and had some options and room to move. Now they say we are bound by the union contract and they treat us like clerks. [Welfare social worker]

I used to be glad I worked in a private agency and wasn't a state worker. I wanted to help people, not be a bureaucrat.

I've been in the children's network for four years, always working myself ragged doing what I could to advocate, coordinate, or somehow make the system work for children. I've been praised by supervisors for my energy, but I still have no security, a low salary, and a sense that the kids I work with are never going to get real help. My friends who can are going to graduate schools or moving. I've got a family and I guess I'm looking for one of those cushy bureaucratic jobs I've always criticized. What else can I do? [Youth worker]

Over and over we heard the complaints—workers in state hospitals felt abandoned and blamed for everything. Halfway house workers saw themselves burning out from lack of support or training or a set of unrealistic expectations. Many at DPW complained of the increasing number of CETA workers in their offices who "don't get training and know they will be gone in a year, so they don't care." While most of the people we interviewed did not themselves express many critical feelings toward clients, all noted increasing hostility toward clients in their work places. Most felt that the climate of general frustration had grown since the early 1970s, as expressed by one worker: "Where I work [a welfare service office] people feel put upon and frustrated with the union, the department, the clients, everything. Last summer when everybody was blaming welfare workers for those murders, it was really bad. We felt like nobody supported us." There are many reasons for all this frustration. The major reforms of the period—deinstitutionalization and the state takeover of welfare—did disrupt old patterns of work, as would the new Department of Social Services. The justification for change was always "better service to clients" but workers often felt forgotten, blamed, and disregarded in the process. Indeed, the need for certain reforms—notably the deinstitutionalization of youth facilities and state hospitals—was often blamed on the presence of an "unreachable" work force.

Union issues played a role in the despair. Boston welfare workers were already organized, under SEIU (Service Employees International Union). State hospital and state school workers had been represented for a while by several AFSCME (American Federation of State, County, and Municipal Employees) and SEIU locals. These locals all had different wage scales and different practices, for human service and nonhuman service workers. In Welfare, the state takeover meant that some workers were organized and some were not. To further add to the disarray, those who had been city workers had the right to bargain collectively but those in state unions did not.

The confusion was intolerable even to a system as unafraid of disorder as Massachusetts state government. In response, the state collective-bargaining laws were amended in 1974 to allow state workers to engage in collective bargaining over wages and benefits with the Commonwealth. Then the task arose of creating a plan for an orderly election and successful negotiations. State unions were fearful of each other. Some—the professors and the nurses—were nervous about open "trade unionism." Finally, with some support from state political activists, the international unions (AFSCME and SEIU) stepped in and proposed an "Alliance" of state employees unions. The Alliance was to run in the 1975 election as a unitary slate and the unions would later divide up the representation of specific state workers among the appropriate SEIU and AFSCME locals. Higher education was removed from the election and nurses were allowed to run unopposed.[13]

Many local unionists reluctantly went along with the proposal devised by their international officers, and approved by the Dukakis administration. As one participant stated:

We were not sure that such a big Alliance would actually help social workers, but if there was to be an election, we needed to win. Without the help of the international leadership, we would not have had the money or the skill to launch a statewide campaign. So we supported it, but remained skeptical.

After the election, a strong victory for the Alliance, the local unions became responsible for defining bargaining units and negotiating a contract. The national staff pulled out—in accordance with an agreement with the local unions that, since they now had expanded dues, they could afford the staff needed to negotiate. The result was a reluctant Alliance, characterized by internal distrust and disagreement over its goals in relation to the administration.

In 1976, a dispute over the first contract led all state workers to stage a brief, illegal strike. The public reaction to this strike was strong and hostile. Media reports and street conversation led many workers to feel despised and unappreciated. One mental health worker summarized a lot of the feelings:

We thought we were performing a needed service. We struck because we felt that management was not treating us right. But people hated us. Even neighbors said sarcastic, snide things about state workers. Everybody seemed to think we were a bunch of deadbeats, getting rich off the state. That, plus the hostility at the [mental health] center afterwards, made me feel really rotten. And the next contract we got wasn't even any better.

When the Alliance was formed, unions gained new members by executive order and an automatic election, not through the consciousness-raising process of an organizing drive. So all were also internally weak as well as distrusting of each other. And the increasing "managerial" focus of most departments under the Dukakis administration meant that all also had to face efforts to limit the issues that were subject to labor-management discussion, under expanding definitions of "management rights." As one union official described the dilemmas:

We should have been able to do more for our members—more internal education, more training. But many of them didn't even really want to join us and they blamed us for a worsening situation in human services. All we could do was to try to keep from falling too far backward in relation to management, but that strategy didn't win many friends or help workers cope with the stress of jobs which became more and more unbearable.

We felt, and often were, helpless.

Conversely, the increase in nonstate, contracted employees also led to a decline in morale. Many people worked for agencies that were totally dependent on the state. Others were in agencies with some state contracts. The uncertainty of year-to-year funding created insecurities, as did the predictability that funding would decline yearly, not increase.

In the early 1970s many young new workers were drawn into the system of community care: day care, halfway houses, and other community services. Such workers were especially visible as contractees of agencies like DYS, DMH, and as nonline OFC employees. Often during these years, such workers were hailed as a "new breed" of committed, nonbureaucratic service workers. As the hassles and the years wore on, these workers left, moved into the bureaucracies for better pay, or went back to school. By 1979 one halfway-house worker could say: "We are institutional workers. We just work in little institutions without even the supports provided by the state hospital. The sense of mission is gone."

Finally, many direct service workers are frustrated by the lack of career mobility within the human service agencies. "The way up is to become management and never see clients," said one welfare worker. And the "management" jobs available were usually not vested with substantial policy-making authority. Many workers saw themselves as forced to become management bureaucrats, to lose the small but important solidarity of other workers, if they wanted advancement. A few even felt used by upper-level management, as did this welfare administrator: "During the strike I was management. I had to cross the picket line or lose my job. But I don't make decisions here. I hated crossing the picket line even more because I didn't have any real power."

All of these pressures have added up during the period under review. It was never wonderful. The National Study Service documented this in 1965. But as the years passed the gap between the heightened rhetoric and the workplace reality seemed to grow. More attention was on the human service agencies than before. Downturns in the economy had made the costs of human service programs more controversial and the new victim to be blamed was the worker along with the old victim, the client.

It is even more difficult to analyze the shifts in recipient status during the period. Welfare militance peaked in the late 1960s and declined steadily as welfare programs became more routinized and as the broad supporting milieu for activism faded. Other client groups, such as the elderly or the handicapped, remained organized but often were drawn into increasingly limited "consumer-advocacy" roles or into legal battles. Many recipients of different services took paraprofessional jobs. Others joined advisory boards. Specific campaigns—for physical access, for Meals on Wheels, against Dukakis's workfare proposal—drew crowds but failed to build ongoing organizations.

Occasional newspaper articles would highlight problems—teenage runaways one week, old people the next, and battered women the week after. But the daily drudgery of surviving the seventies was hard to capture, perhaps because it was so unchanging. As one woman reflected:

It's a full-time job, being on welfare. You spend your days in lines, waiting for food stamps, waiting at the clinic, waiting for a redetermination. The department loses your birth certificate so you have to go get a copy, have it copied and go back to the office.

Your children have hassles in school, your housing is falling apart. You have to find the cheap store to shop. The days all blur together and it's hard to remember what happened, when, and if it was ever any worse or if it's getting better.

One old-time organizer has come to the conclusion that little has changed:

I remember when, because of the movement, it was nothing to be ashamed of, to be on welfare. If you needed it, women supported you, liberals wanted to listen to you, churches and community groups recognized the need. Now all that's gone. People make comments when you use your food stamps in the grocery line. Women are embarrassed again. It's almost like nothing happened, nothing at all.

Another young welfare organizer disagreed, however. Her comments are more typical of those people we interviewed and seem to suggest some hope:

When we try to organize now, people come us and say: "I was at the Grove Hall demonstration back in the sixties, can I help even if I'm not on welfare?" And more women have used their benefits to go to school and get skills than was so back then. So things are bad, and in some ways worse, but they are in more ways better.

We can learn from NWRO not just to rely on individual strategies like they did. We are trying to make alliances with other poor peoples' issues like housing. We don't have a big movement or the spirit of the 1960s, but I think we have more skills to fight with.

5   The Department of Public Welfare as "Designated Patient"

The notion of "designated patient" comes from theories of family interaction. Often one member of a disturbed family is defined by everyone in the family as "the patient," the "sick" member of an otherwise healthy system. All the difficulties, tensions, and contradictions within the family are played out as symptoms in this "designated patient." The patient's actual difficulties are masked by the web of problems he or she "presents" for other family members. Recovery for the entire family depends upon helping the "patient" give up his or her familiar role, thereby forcing other family members to exhibit their own symptoms. In the course of change the whole family may experience "breakdown." Everyone, including the falsely defined "patient," must flounder until he or she arrives at a new, healthier role.

Our interviews and research revealed that the Welfare Department has been the designated patient of the Massachusetts human services system. As some "family members" put it: "I work for OFC instead of Welfare because they are a dead agency. There's no hope for them over there. They are all impossible bureaucrats"; or "Mental Health has been flexible in many areas. We've tried hard to work cooperatively with Welfare, but they block our every move because they are terrified of any change"; or "Our Area Strategy team would be fine if it weren't for Welfare. They just won't cooperate with anybody. All they worry about are their rules and regulations and they fear any kind of change."

And from the "patient," we've listened to people tell us: "Everybody hates us. The clients blame us for everything. The public and the press assume we are to blame for every child abuse and fraud case. Our own commissioner talks about how bad everything and everyone is in the department"; or "The other agencies think we are backward and stupid for not giving them everything they want. But they aren't responsible for accounting for the money and the recipients like we are. They aren't the people everyone assumes are incompetent and impossible. If anything does wrong anywhere with anybody poor in Massachusetts, we take the blame."

Such perceptions create self-fulfilling prophecies. Welfare workers feel under siege and unappreciated, so they lose energy. Other agencies can avoid their own difficulties because it is "always worse at Welfare." The money keeps flowing and the programs keep operating but no one takes any joy in the disbursal or any sense of accomplishment in the delivery of service. One assistance payments worker summed up the problem this way:

How do I like my work? I'll tell you, it's a weird job. They would be happy with me if all my "cases" were closed, but then I couldn't have a job. I'm supposed to be very, very sure the person is not cheating somehow. But if I do find some problem, it causes me so much trouble I feel like it would have been easier to keep quiet—except that I might get in trouble if somebody else finds out. There is very little to do that's really rewarding. I usually can't win for losing.

This chapter explores the symptoms of this designated patient and examines the major implications of the past fourteen years. In doing so we will often refer back to, or elaborate on, events presented in chapter 3. The goal is to understand more of the workings of the Welfare Department and to explain something of the dynamic discussed by one mid-level welfare administrator:

The Welfare Department is different from other state agencies, bad as they are. For one thing, we are always apologizing, always talking about how bad things are. I don't think it's only, like the social work schools say, because of our clients. I think it's something else. Like in this society everybody has to be independent, to take care of themselves and their own. Just by our name we represent what everybody—professionals, the public, the legislators—is most afraid of, "going over the hill to the poor house." People *want* to see us as bad and as dehumanizing; otherwise why are they working so hard to stay off welfare? It gets really bad when our own staff feel the same way. So I think it's hopeless. As long as we do what we do it will never get better.

Repercussions of Reform: The State Takeover

One way to view the history of the Welfare Department during this period is to see it as undergoing the natural cycle of reaction and readjustment that follows major organizational reform.

As we noted in chapter 3, the legislature passed only a state takeover proposal. Despite pleas from Commissioner Ott, there was little attention paid to the administrative structures needed to implement the new system—or to the possible supports required for the new department, suddenly the biggest in the state, to operate effectively.

Simple administrative processes became massive problems. Many cities and towns had different systems of record keeping. There were widespread stories of the shoe boxes full of (unpaid) Medicaid bills which arrived in the commissioner's office on July 1, 1968. Disbursement of welfare checks and paychecks became major tasks. Some cities and towns switched personnel at the last minute, so that the new department found itself with 5,500 new employees, some of whom were rejects from city and town governments with little experience. Everyone who recalled the period for us stressed the confusion:

Plan? Sure we planned, but our "planning" involved discovering the names of employees and recipients, dealing with unhappy employees, recipients, and Medicaid vendors. We had no time for training new workers or instituting new systems. We had no new staff or money to implement the takeover, so all we could do was to try to keep the files organized. Many of the local officials had no loyalty to the new system, some even seemed to want it to fail. [State official]

All I remember is confusion, a whole lot of new names and papers. Nobody knew quite what had changed and what was still the same. Everybody was afraid of doing the wrong thing and not sure what the right thing was. [Worker]

The takeover made it easier for us in some ways. We could go straight to the commissioner and the governor with our complaints and they couldn't tell us it wasn't their responsibility. [Organizer]

We had been raising hell in our local office, with MAWs. Then they told us they couldn't do anything any more; we had to go to the state. We weren't sure what that meant, but if Commissioner Ott wanted to talk to us, we'd oblige. Of course when we got there, he didn't know what was happening either. [Welfare activist]

Without computers, extra money, or even a strong management approach, the department floundered and never really appeared under control until late 1970, when a new commissioner and the new flat-grant system lent an illusion of order to the still reeling bureaucracy.

The internal management problems and the difficulties of dealing for the first time with a union and with strong welfare rights agitation made the new department vulnerable. So too did the amount of information regarding state welfare expenditures which became more obvious with the new structure. One political analyst called the new situation "a set up":

Before, welfare costs were somewhat hidden, associated with local budgets. Cities and towns felt identified, for better or worse, with their local welfare office, so politicians felt some need for restraint in criticizing the system. With the takeover, and the simultaneous, but unrelated, increase in welfare rolls and Medicaid costs, no one felt a need to protect the department in the public eye. The lack of planning time and money assured bureaucratic disaster. And the lack of a respected constituency—even the professionals abandoned welfare—left the agency in *big* trouble.

Looking back, we can see that a state takeover was probably necessary, given costs and complexities of programs. But the state instituted it exactly opposite from the planned, careful way recommended by the National Study Service. As a result, the department suffered an institutional shock from which it only began to recover ten years later.

A Manageable AFDC Program

Throughout this period, as we have seen, the call was for better management of welfare. During the Sargent years it was for better *management systems*, a better structure of the department, reduction in the AFDC error rate, improvement in income reporting, payments, and eligibility systems, the creation of a computerized management-information system. After 1974, the emphasis expanded to include the demand for *more managers*, for more experts in the system who would know how to set up, implement, and evaluate the needed system as well as make sure that they were in place.

AFDC was the target of most of this call for better management and managers—although Medicaid experienced it also. The first effort was the successful implementation of the flat grant program which was meant to eliminate waste and privilege from the old special-needs program—to stop the ability of organized client groups to be "squeaky wheels" and thereby get more than their share.

The way in which the flat grant was introduced was indicative of management efforts under Steven Minter. The first program, although a management victory, was loose and still allowed many discretionary areas for the eligibility worker. But the goal of uniformity had been established. The next four years saw a gradual decline in the number of discretionary categories, and a subsequent increase in management control.

After the flat grant victory, the department proceeded in its efforts at administrative reform. Each time there was a similar strategy of establishing the administrative principles of new programs and then gradually strengthening the "reform." Work Incentive Programs (WIN) were instituted but seldom enforced as such, and only gradually were they to become the "forced work" feared by early opponents. Different consulting firms were asked to suggest new administrative structures and computer systems, but although they were instituted with much fanfare, the results of most of these studies and projects were disappointing.

It was not until the end of 1972 that the department's advisory board could proclaim that "state administration becomes a reality" because one computer center was sending out checks, the regional offices were strengthened, and many administrative processes were becoming centralized and standardized. Indeed, it was not until its 1974 *Annual Report* that the department was willing to claim major administrative victories, such as the final separation of services and payments, the internal restructure of the department, and a reduced error rate.

Over the years there was increasing public and legislative pressure on the department to reduce AFDC error rates and to hold down costs. Each year brought legislative efforts to reduce costs and benefit levels, most of which were resisted by the Sargent administration but were later supported by the Dukakis administration. Hiring freezes were imposed and increases in benefits were denied. Federal pressures, resulting from lawsuits, helped overcome some hiring difficulties, but the ever-present pressures regarding "the welfare mess" constantly put the department on the defensive. A major administrative success of the Sargent years—the relatively smooth transition of old age and disability programs to the federally sponsored SSI program—did not even help the department. By taking away a program for the "worthy poor" the institution of SSI left the Welfare Department with even fewer constituents deemed "deserving" by the general public—and the General Court.

As we have seen, serious cuts were made in the first Dukakis year. Although these cuts were defended in the name of the "budget crisis," and some were later abandoned, their early institution set the tone for the management approach of the Stevens/Sharp administration. Computer systems began to be established and the management-information system was finally instituted.

Different forms of workplace organization were tried and attempts were made to redefine caseloads and to establish caseload quotas. Many people were hired with MBA's and placed in regional as well as state offices.

The result of the ten years of administrative development that followed the state takeover of welfare was a more "managed" system—if not a more manageable one. Welfare caseloads stabilized, the error rate diminished, as did worker autonomy. One long-time worker in the department summed up the situation:

> The whole thing is more under control now. It still feels messy and too full of paperwork, but people know what they are supposed to do, whether they like it or not. After the takeover, for a long time, we sometimes didn't know who the clients were or how much they should get. Now we know that, although we still don't have time to see them or the resources to help in any way besides the minimum budget. Is this what you would call progress?

Medicaid

When the Medicaid program (Title XIX of the Social Security Act) first began in Massachusetts, it was one of the most extensive programs in the country. All areas of eligibility were pushed to their limits, against the advice of Commissioner Ott, who called for a slower process of gradual expansion of the existing medical assistance benefits. Ott and others argued that the existing medical assistance program, when viewed in conjunction with the extensive clinic programs of many (especially Boston-area) hospitals, provided an adequate system of health care for most poor people. They argued that institutions and professionals would benefit more from a rapid, undermanaged expansion than recipients would.

Overruled, the department found itself with an extremely small central staff and a rapidly growing program by the takeover in 1968. Indeed, besides an effort to coordinate billing and accounting procedures, every Medicaid director during the period had to fight for more staff at the central level.

The Medicaid program, although described by some as the "forgotten program" of the department, became one of its first major links to the outside world. Long before the department began purchasing services, or "coordinating" under mandate with other agencies, the Medicaid program became involved—with little direction or guidance—with many other areas of the public and private sectors: the Department of Health and Mental Health, the

Medical Association, the hospitals and the Nursing Home Association. Efficient billing procedures remained a perpetual issue, as did contracting and managing an expensive system where 60–70 percent of the costs went to the hospitals and nursing homes in Massachusetts by 1978. Beginning with the directorship of Mel Scovell (1973–1976), the program began to play a more active role in setting standards and defining appropriate care. Scovell, especially, was known for his consumer approach, described by one co-worker, a Medicaid administrator: "Scovil used to manufacture shoes. He looked at Medicaid from a new perspective. Instead of apologizing to the hospital doctors and nursing homes because we were so disorganized, he said to them—'Hey, we pay you millions of dollars a year, what are we getting for our money?' "

Under this leadership, the Welfare Department also began to play a major role in financing deinstitutionalization. Extensive negotiations allowed DPW and DMH officials to come to agreements which meant that the placement of patients in nursing homes or community residences would be covered by Medicaid. As one welfare official noted: "Those were delicate times. People didn't realize that there could have been no significant deinstitutionalization if Welfare had been obstructionist or foot dragging." Similar, if less dramatic, negotiations also were important in creating good relationships with Department of Elderly Affairs and its Home Care Corporations.

By 1978, Medicaid was no longer an ignored program, fighting for recognition even while accounting for a major proportion of the department's expenditures. As social services were being transferred to a new agency, Medicaid was even becoming the "area of choice" for many workers within the department.

Social Services: From Stepchild to New Agency

As we have seen, striking changes occurred in the social services during this period. Prior to the state takeover, and for a few years thereafter, services remained the same—mainly protective services, foster care, and adoption services.[1] Day care and homemaker services were available on a case-by-case basis. Although there were superficial state service plans, there was little interest in planning an expansion of service programs.

By Minter's tenure the state delivery of services had not changed but, by 1974, the department had begun to spend a large portion of its service budget on services purchased from community agencies. This increased purchasing was expanded even further with the support of Title XX regulations in 1975. With pressure from the executive office, the department was forced to become more involved with other state agencies. The planning, training, and contracting activities necessary to administering Title XX forced Welfare into one "coordinated" activity after another. Like it or not, Welfare Department officials found themselves in the informed public eye as never before.

In short, by 1977, the social services branch of the department had become critically involved, like the Medicaid program, with all other human service providers in the state. A glance at any of the Title XX plans shows the level of purchase involved—up to 80 percent of the entire Title XX service allocation—and our interviews confirmed this emerging role: "We have to depend on the Welfare Department for contracts and cooperation in many areas. I can't say that they are often very cooperative or energetic. We always have to push for everything" (Mental health center worker); or "Training is a good example of departmental limits. While there are, indeed, lots of built-in problems with the program, Welfare people made it worse by being so bureaucratic and unimaginative! (DYS administrator). In their defense, Welfare service and training staff argued that other agencies did not understand or respect the regulatory pressures they were under: "We are the designated agency, not anybody else. We take the heat and make the headlines if anything goes wrong. Sure, that makes us more cautious."

These and other pressures, as we have seen, led to the establishment of a new social service agency in 1978. The final separation of services from welfare leaves the old agency with the chance to concentrate on managing the expensive income and medical assistance programs, without the "distraction" of service provision. The new agency is faced with the opportunity to create a program for the delivery and monitoring of the major social service efforts across the Commonwealth. One new DSS employee described the challenge: "Now we'll see how much of the problems with services resulted from the old Welfare paralysis and how much is inherent in the social services network itself. We have a chance to improve the contracting system and to see how much can be done about child abuse. It's exciting and frightening at the same time."

Can This Agency Be Saved?

Will splitting the designated patient in two solve problems—or double them?

The structural constraints remain. The Medicaid program still links the Welfare Department to other agencies. Its clients are still the people most eligible for other public programs, and most in the spotlight when budget cutters want to attack "illegitimate" beneficiaries of the public dole. So its central role in the Massachusetts service system will continue, regardless of the loss of service programs.

Two broad choices may be open to welfare officials. On the one hand, the most likely choice is that drawn from past experience. Welfare officials can continue to be troubled and unable to stem the rising tide of inflation and pressure for fiscal austerity. They can passively take up whatever federal initiatives come down from Washington and then force other agencies to go along with such punitive priorities. Thus, progressive public and professional hostility can remain focused on the chronic, self-designated patient.

However, another option is theoretically possible, if the patient truly wished to improve. An open admission could be made that the department was pleased to provide money, medical services, and food stamps to those in need. Such "services" could be valued for themselves by the department and organizational energy directed toward the efficiency and sensitivity with which services were delivered. Workers could be praised for performing a basic social function, rather than punished for only dealing with money, instead of with more caring services. In today's hard times, the Welfare Department could assume a new identity as the place where people get what they most need—money—instead of its old identity as a place where only poor, miserable people go to be kept alive. The department might even be able to admit out loud that its purpose can be neither to end poverty nor to punish people for being poor, but to provide needed temporary relief to the worst pains of modern life.[2]

Such an approach would break the rules of the Circle Game. Other agencies would have to change if the designated patient stopped playing its well-known role. DSS might be free to admit that its social workers can never solve child abuse but that perhaps they could help create a network of community services to help if abuse arises. Clients and workers might begin to feel less harassed and abused by the system. Other agencies might have to confront their own inadequacies as well as their involvement in past problems. A system where there is no designated patient might make everyone—except the patient—look a little worse, but it might be one where people could get a little work done rather than constantly looking for someone else to blame.

6 Power and Protection: Dynamics of the System

As we have seen, Massachusetts human service agencies comprise an unstable and often unhappy system. Since the members were all identified, in 1972, the rules have generally been those of a zero-sum (another circle?) game. A loss for Welfare meant a gain for Mental Health, or a gain for Elderly Affairs resulted in a loss for the Executive Office of Human Services. It helps to understand the special role the Welfare Department held as designated patient, but the full dynamic can only be more fully understood by examining the shifting places of the other agencies within the system. We must look, especially, for the power that each agency was able to exert over the others and the degree to which each was able to protect its major programs. Again, the overview of program developments has already been presented in chapter 3. Here we focus on the emerging and changing relationships among agencies.

The Secretariat: Aborted Reform

Francis Sargent's efforts to reorganize state government into a cabinet system were a limited success, with some unexpected results.

The Commonwealth was left with a half-hearted reorganization, one in which the power of the secretariats was defined almost totally by the personal influence of each secretary and the individual willingness of the governor to accept the advice of his chief officers. In human services, the picture is further clouded by the last minute creation of a tenth secretariat, the Office of Elderly Affairs. While the secretariat of Human Services is by far the largest in terms of control of state resources, the establishment of Elderly Affairs is a graphic sign that it does not represent all the human service clients or agencies within the Commonwealth.

The different styles of the three EOHS secretaries during the period under study offer a clear example of the potential and limits of the cabinet office to influence the Massachusetts system of human services. Under Peter Goldmark, the new office tried to create an activist image and a sense of energy for a set of commissioners, agencies, and boards over which it had no statutory control. Joint planning was supported, deinstitutionalization and improvements in children's programs were pushed. Although there was little overt obstruction by the major agencies—Welfare, Mental Health, Corrections, and Health—a strong sense remained that the secretariat was glamorous but weak and could do little to force changes in the entrenched agencies. One senior-level administrator put it this way:

Goldmark could look good with the press and talk a good game about innovation, integration, and coordinated planning. In the end, however, he knew that he couldn't force his way on anything, so he always tried to present the secretariat as leading the commissioners in the direction they had already chosen to go.

Goldmark's difficulty with the legislature, cited by many commentators as a "problem," was mild compared to the political problems encountered by Lucy Benson, the first secretary under Dukakis (1975–January 1976). Although her brief tenure was not notable for programmatic reasons, it does support the idea that the personal influence of the secretary is a key to power. Benson found herself without a set of programmatic goals and without a constituency; she had neither the clout to gain support from the governor and the legislature nor the ability to influence commissioners below her. Her unlamented departure left many wondering if the secretariat could be a feasible base from which to influence the policy and programmatic direction of human services in Massachusetts.

The regime of Jerald Stevens answered that question affirmatively. Stevens continued with a small staff but instituted "policy groups" which brought together high-level administrators from different agencies in an attempt to encourage, push, and support them in more coordinated efforts. Stevens's crisp (even cold) managerial style was more supportive of administrative redesign than of programmatic pleas for improved service. But in many areas he re-established EOHS as an important element in the definition of human services in Massachusetts. He also continued a trend, begun by Goldmark, of serving as a buffer between the commissioners and human service advocates. Under a strong secretary, the commissioners (of Welfare, Mental Health, or whatever) could appear to serve as budgetary and program advocates, responsive to the demands of consumers and the community. The secretary, then, could play the "bad-guy" role previously forced directly on the commissioners; he could insist on cuts to comply with the governor's budget or on abandonment of pet reforms. Less susceptible to direct pressure, the nay-saying secretary could, literally, take the heat off the commissioners, an important task if there was to be stability in upper-level management.

Goldmark's administration also proved that the secretary could play an important role when commissioners get into trouble. With Greenblatt, Miller, and Corrections Commissioner Boone, Goldmark helped to plan a strategy for dealing with public attacks and was able to help plan more controlled leave-taking when commissioners were forced to resign. One political analyst noted:

Goldmark kept Jerry Miller alive longer than would have been possible if the governor had been forced to make the decision alone. He tried to deal with internal critics and to help plan a defense strategy. Finally, the pressure was too much, and Miller became a political liability. But Miller had an extra six months to work.

The failure of Area Strategy, however, shows the limits of a secretary's ability to influence program decisions. Stevens committed EOHS and the Social Services Policy Committee to the effort of shifting decision making and planning downward (and, some would argue, weakening existing agencies) into area communities. Stevens was a strong secretary but he was not strong enough to force such a drastic, unified policy direction on unwilling agencies. Still, one of Stevens's legacies is that an area-based strategy remains at the heart of the new Social Services agency and helps define organizational questions for human services even after the original projects fade.

In short, six years of an Executive Office of Human Service did not profoundly affect the delivery of services in the Commonwealth, but it did institute a level of government that can influence the course of services planning and that can be an important aspect of the development of a system. As one ex-official put it: "On a day-to-day level the secretariat has little influence or impact most of the time. But commissioners and their staff can be forced to communicate and pressured to consider other agencies and their programs. Considering how isolated everyone was before, that's some progress."

All three secretaries found their major battles were with the secretaries of Administration and Finance (A & F), all of whom were key advisers to the governor. In each case, problems arose from the need to gain access to the governor and acceptance of budget decisions made within the secretariat. Frustration with these pressures led Stevens to resign and were acknowledged as serious problems by Goldmark and Benson. Power for an EOHS secretary depends on persuasion and on creating a sense that one has the support of the governor. Limiting access to the governor threatens the secretary's ability to influence commissioners. Lack of support for secretariat budget proposals has a similar effect. Thus, a final lesson from this period is an understanding that the strength of the secretary of Human Services depends on the maintenance of a working noncompetitive relationship with the secretary of Administration and Finance—no easy task in the world of high-stakes Massachusetts politics.

Leadership for Mental Health

Before deinstitutionalization, the Department of Mental Health held a respected, if unexciting, position in relation to other state agencies. It employed a large staff on substantial property and was led by prestigious professionals. The task for the department, once deinstitutionalization was decided upon, was to change its direction without losing ground. This meant meeting two goals. First, the department had to find other funding for its ex-patients and residents or the costs of deinstitutionalization would be prohibitive. Here, as we have seen, the department was highly successful. Arrangements were made for SSI or GR coverage of clients leaving hospitals and for Medicaid and Title XX coverage of medical and social service costs. Contact was made with Massachusetts Rehabilitation and pressure put on it to serve more mentally ill and retarded clients. In short, the leadership exerted in this coordinating effort was essential if the department was to succeed in its publicly proclaimed goal of full deinstitutionalization by the 1980s.

Second, as state hospitals and schools were emptied, the agency was forced to look for new roles and new approaches for its staff. Eager social workers and community mental health workers began scanning local communities, looking for appropriate activities. They found them in schools, nursing homes, local community groups. It was only natural that the staff of the department whose clients had gone to the community would become community leaders, and even community advocates.[1]

In other states across the country, deinstitutionalization has brought interagency warfare between mental health and welfare agencies—witnessing fights over dollars, accountability, and "ownership" of clients. In Massachusetts the weakness of the Welfare Department, its preoccupation with fiscal and administrative concerns, and the lack of professional credentials among its staff left the field open to DMH. The institution of the new Department of Social Services may, in the 1980s, lead to some future conflicts, but, in all likelihood, "the horse is out of the barn." In 1980, $11 million in Medicaid expenditures went for mental health costs. Another $11 million from Title XX were for mental health services. These numbers, coupled with the steady state support for DMH, shows an impressive pattern of bureaucratic ascendancy during this period.[2]

There was opposition to deinstitutionalization over the years but it was not well focused. Individual communities protested community residences in their area. Professionals often fretted aloud about the lack of adequate care for people coming out of facilities, or about the misleading "revolving-door" effect, where clients are simply admitted more often, for shorter periods. But it was difficult to launch a full attack without appearing to support the large state institutions, which were universally discredited.

Indeed, a final measure of the power of DMH is the way that it was able to keep public attention turned to the abuses in its remaining state facilities. Like the welfare leadership, DMH officials have been willing to parade their difficulties before the legislature and the public in order to get funds, but they always exposed problems in the institutions, not in the community facilities. Instead, the community facilities were always praised, with few of their difficulties surfacing for the press, the public, or the General Court.

In this manner, DMH was able to "have it both ways." It kept public criticism and debate spotlighted on its dwindling, increasingly unloved institutions, while at the same time deflected criticisms of community programs with the argument that they were "so much better than state hospitals." One mental-health professional expressed the dilemma in this way:

I'm for good services. Whenever I complain about poor care in the community, they tell me how much better things are than in the schools and hospitals. When I complain about the hospitals and ask for improvements, they tell me they don't want to invest money there, they want to move people out. Somehow it feels like the old shell game.

Or the old Circle Game?

The Department of Youth Services:
Teaching the Effects of Reform

Unlike the situation in the Department of Mental Health, deinstitutionalization was accomplished quickly and almost totally at the Department of Youth Services. The costs of change, as we have seen, were great, in terms of staff morale and backlash from many communities and some professionals. The years since Miller left have seen the department retreat from some of its more experimental programs and institute some increases in secure facilities. However, the major programmatic advances have not yet been turned back. As one DYS official summed up the change in early 1979:

> Our problems now are different. We don't have to wage the big battles that Miller did. Now we have to coordinate among the contracted programs and with other state agencies. We have to monitor programs better and deal with the question of violent kids.
> We may have to give up some goals, but we'll never go back to the jails. That's progress.

Other agencies, particularly the Welfare Department, have felt the crunch from the changes in DYS. Children who were once incarcerated were turned back to DPW for foster care. In 1973, the Children in Need of Services Legislation pushed Welfare into providing for children previously seen as delinquent and under the jurisdiction of Youth Services. And, often as important, the impassioned new youth workers at DYS became a common source of public criticism for the Welfare Department. They were, in one official's words, "untrained advocates" who had not yet become "civil servants," and who did not understand "bureaucratic reality." At the public hearings which were mandated by Title XX, DYS employees and contracted agency staff would be "unruly" and "unprofessional," a style left unpunished by DYS leadership.

Other agencies learned a great deal from the growth pains of DYS. Especially Mental Health, but also DPW and OFC learned about the ways to develop new contracted agencies as well as ways to use existing ones. They watched Miller fight battles on all fronts, with unions, staff, clients, and other agencies, and many reasoned that the price of drastic reform was too high. Some also learned that the work of a state agency that administers many contracted programs is very different from one that delivers its own services. In the words of one mental health official, these were all vital lessons: "We didn't do a big study, but we did watch DYS flounder and struggle. We would discuss how hard it was and how it could be done better. Those discussions would come back when we planned our own deinstitutionalization. They did us a big favor by going first."

Patterns for Other Agencies

The Office for Children was never able to gain a solid footing during this period because it remained split between service and advocacy. Therefore, if anything, its role in the interagency jostle was to show the importance of advocacy for a quick public following, but its limits as a way to build a strong bureaucratic base. Similarly, its work as a catalyst to make sure that Chapter 766 was really enacted by local schools also won friends among parents but little support from established local officials who felt unable to afford the financial drain of bringing special education into the schools.

The ultimate and most significant effect of OFC activity may be that it reinforced the importance of social services as a desirable commodity. In 1978, unlike 1966, there were state-supported agencies out in local communities helping people demand services, questioning the quality of state and local programs. Such activity leads to a more widespread sense that services have become a "right," as compared to the "treatment" they were considered to be in 1966.

On the other hand, the Department of Elder Affairs has shown that a service and coordinating agency can serve the interests of one constituency. The department has proven that a smaller agency, especially under its own secretariat, can bargain effectively with welfare and other state officials to secure acceptable regulations and service for its constituency. Although the privileged status of elders as worthy of claims on public money surely helped, the major source of DEA's success seems to stem from its ability to balance service with moderate advocacy.

Although many welfare officials and other human service observers originally viewed DEA as just another agency wanting something from Welfare and fighting limited battles, the practice of the department has changed their opinion. After SSI was instituted, DPW was even less involved in elder affairs and without the pressure of DEA might have been even more forgetful of older citizens. A former state official summed up many comments on DEA:

"The conventional wisdom at the time [of the state reorganization] was that agencies should be organized by function, not constituency. DEA showed us all that, without special treatment, old people would always be forgotten. I think a lot of people have learned something from their success."

One final agency deserves mention here, although it was not discussed in the historical narrative. The Massachusetts Rehabilitation Commission (Mass. Rehab) continued with little change from 1966 until 1978. Its mandate and activities changed only slightly. Pressure from Mental Health forced its attention to a limited number of new clients. The implementation of SSI has involved MRC in expanded determinations of disability. But this small agency continued to rely heavily on its federal funding throughout the period and to remain a cooperative but inactive contributor to the myriad of interagency change efforts. It serves as an example of what might have happened to all human service agencies in Massachusetts in another time, with less volatile actors.

Provider Power

The number of private agencies receiving state money to deliver services increased dramatically during the twelve years under review. One consequence of this, as we have seen, was a decrease in credibility for the "private sector" as an unbiased advocate for human services. Another outcome was that provider agencies, working through the Massachusetts Council for Human Service Providers and other advocacy groups, lobbied for themselves and sought uniformity from Welfare and other departments in regard to standard setting and contract terms, as well as program definitions. In this way providers, again, moved from being advocates for clients to being advocates for themselves.

Labor issues, also, have affected this network of private contracted agencies, as has been mentioned earlier. Workers in small contracted agencies were often paid less and less well throughout the seventies, yet they often experienced greater flexibility and autonomy in their jobs than state workers. These quality-of-work issues were often valued highly by a predominantly young, "unprofessional" work force. Workers in contracted agencies lacked union benefits and were even seen by union members as threatening the unions' power over state working conditions. Yet the complexities of the contracting structure make the hope of organizing contracted agencies seem bleak, except in the largest proprietary (profit-making) agencies. Although the bureaucratic rules required by Title XX regulations made it easier to be a large private agency than a small one, the majority of agencies remained still small enough to make union organizing a difficult and complex task.

In spite of the growth of "private" agencies there has been little solid program evaluation of the benefits of contracted services. Most Welfare Department efforts to "monitor" focused on fiscal accountability and on evaluating quantity—not quality—of services delivered. This situation created another dilemma for the conscientious service provider:

We actually would like a solid evaluation of our performance, of what we do well and what we could do better. But we can't trust the Welfare Department to do this, because they only seem to care about money and not about what it takes to provide a good service. Since we can't trust them, we have to sound negative about their evaluation schemes, but we get hurt too, because we don't know if what we are doing is right or wrong. [Day care director]

A System for What?

I don't know what's the matter with me. I went to the hearing to listen to all the positions on the proposed bill. Many people spoke from different agencies and they seemed to think they were disagreeing with each other. And I guess they were. But to me they all looked and sounded alike. Try as I might, I couldn't understand the differences; all I saw was a bunch of well-dressed people, speaking the same language. [Student researcher]

In many ways the powerful administrators who oversee the agencies discussed here form a privileged "fraternity," an elite who move in and out of jobs with the ebb and flow of governors, secretaries, and commissioners.[3] They all know each other; they go to each other's parties. Despite their struggles for power, and their efforts to protect their agencies and personal reputations, they seldom offer a discussion of strong—common or competing—substantive goals. Instead, interviews and party chit-chat focus on whose program is being cut, who got what grant, or who is moving to another agency. In the face of such an environment, it becomes almost rude to discuss the impact of programs on clients or on workers. Attempts at such discussion seem strangely out of place, automatically marking the initiator as an outsider.

Of course, such observations can be, and have been, made about the movers and shakers within any large bureaucratic system. The task remains to look beyond all the personal and organizational jockeying to answer the question, "power for what?" [4] Why do all these people act the way they do, and could it be different?

Obviously, we cannot fully answer such questions here. But the beginnings of answers start to suggest themselves, especially if we return to one of our basic assumptions, that a root cause of the Circle Game is the failure of participants to admit to the limits of what can be accomplished by social programs in this society. What we see, as we watch all the upper-level administrators interact, is the natural result of a collective denial that the programs in which these professionals have invested so much are so very limited in basic effect. Everyone responds by personalizing discussions: it is not programs but individuals who fail. A few practice denial by taking the narrow, offensive position: deinstitutionalization becomes, by assertion, the one policy that could work for everyone and only fails because others fail to support it. More often, administrators play the denial game by a general defensive posture: we won't risk a lot; we'll wait, watch other programs, and then blame our problems on whoever is the most public failure of the moment. A recent variant is the "manager's lament": we could have succeeded if only we had a better information system, or data base, or managerial capacity.

Because the range of tactics is so limited, it is no surprise that the student quoted above could be confused. Few can risk clear language or dare talking in a public forum. Better to be thought a bureaucrat, or even stupid, than to say something too clearly and be exposed as a services professional without a solution. Those few who break the rules, like a Jerry Miller in DYS, or a Robert Curtis in Area Strategy, are out quickly, despite their effectiveness.

Yet, is it really so weak to say that, although poverty still exists and will continue to exist, some people were able to live with a little more dignity during this period? Is one's professional efficacy so threatened by admitting to the notion that some crazy people need institutions sometimes and some don't and that we don't know why? Or, are we so illegitimate if we acknowledge that we have no idea how to cure child abuse in this society? Perhaps, if someone had broken out of the Circle Game long enough to say such things, then the public would have fewer illusions and would be more tolerant of the inherent "failures" in the system. They might also have been able to support reasonable changes within the system, rather than come to distrust all changes as costly failure. Instead, the system is consistently defended by those who feel that they must misrepresent it in order to keep their personal and professional power. Its underlying goals are thereby discredited

and many acquire the attitudes of the welfare mother we interviewed: "I know we need welfare programs and all that, but sometimes I just wish they were gone, no matter what. All those
agencies and their promises, when they can't really do anything
for you but make you feel bad about what you don't have."

7   The Ties That Bind:
1966–1978

As we argued earlier, remembering can be too painful without understanding. Our brief examination of how the Circle Game worked for Massachusetts human services has suggested both that there is much to remember and that understanding is very difficult. The purpose of this chapter is to review what has changed and what stayed the same, and to begin to suggest what it all may mean.

Some Things Change

Our survey of the history suggests that there *is* change within the Circle Game. The frustrations and dead ends are there, but so too are important changes. This is no static system. Perhaps we need to see it as the rolling circle we postulated in chapter 1. Or what is important may be that changes be recognized, acknowledged, and evaluated. In the day-to-day hassles of service work, even great changes can be lost in the shuffle of never-ending paper and pressure, which surely does not change.

Organizational changes

Reorganizations have created a more centralized system since 1966. Both the big reorganization into the secretariat and the extensive internal agency restructurings have created a network of programs that looks different and still offers the hope for more accountability than existed sixteen years ago. For example, the Welfare Department offers comparable, if disliked, service to people with the same problems from Boston to Chicopee. DSS has filled a gap in leadership for children's programs, despite the weakness of OFC. There is still fragmentation and "falling through the cracks" for older people, but at least there is one state agency to complain to.

A comparison of the two organizational charts (1966 and the present, charts 1 and 2) undeniably shows a system that makes more sense, on paper at least.

On the negative side, reorganization has, as critics always assert, added another level of bureaucracy to the system. Try as we might, we could find no figures to suggest how many administrators have been added to human service agencies since 1966. Our sense, shared by everyone we interviewed, is that there was substantial growth in the number of administrators relative to the number of direct service staff. While we would not dispute the need for adequate staff (especially in programs like Medicaid where a major state responsibility is to monitor other programs), many agencies do seem "top heavy" with people who have little program experience. One social worker described a typical situation in her comments concerning a mental health center:

We used to work together pretty well at the center. Then they decided we needed more structure, more "definition of tasks." Maybe we did. So they studied us and then hired a management team to tell us what we could and could not do. These people seemed to know nothing of *what* we did, but they seemed perfectly comfortable telling us *how* to do it.

Another negative aspect of reorganization has been mentioned earlier. The presence of an EOHS secretary has protected governors and commissioners from hostility resulting from budget and program cuts. Sometimes under Goldmark and Stevens, a welfare or mental health commissioner could push for a budget that reflected the demands of many constituencies. He could play the role of program advocate. After being overruled by the secretary, the commissioner could go back to his constituency (either inside or outside the department) and tell war stories about how hard he fought, and lost. The trouble here is that the commissioner and the secretary were really on the same team, so the fight was rigged. (Of course, use of this strategy depends on the presence of a system able to tolerate at least the appearance of diversity, which may not always be present, given the egos of some governors or some secretaries.)

Similarly, Governor Sargent established a practice of referring all complaints to his secretary, so the governor's office was less vulnerable to daily pressure. Some would even argue that this was the major reason Sargent wanted a cabinet.[1] Dukakis followed Sargent's lead, often acting like a star baseball player who will only speak through his agent. The trouble is that we have yet to find an EOHS Secretary with the autonomy and ability of Jerry Kapstein, the infamous high-stakes baseball agent.

The development of a management approach to human services is another change from 1966. At that time few people, even at the top levels of agencies, would have called themselves managers. Ott was a social worker; Greenblatt a psychiatrist; Coughlin an educator and juvenile corrections official. Program evaluators and critics referred to the need for better administration and coordination, but the sense that "management" was needed at every level of human services delivery—from the case manager to the commissioner—had not evolved. It emerged, as we have seen, with support from the Nixon administration. The entrance of a new breed of human service professional into agency life and the concurrent increase in public service unionism also helped to bring about the management thrust.[3]

With this shift, many of the long-standing problems facing human service agencies—i.e., increasing caseloads, adequate tracing of clients—were redefined as "management problems." A new approach to human service thereby grew up. Real management problems, such as the needs for proper record-keeping systems or appropriate and predictable expenditure of funds, became mixed up with difficulties that arose from the need to respond to the extreme problems of human service clients, such as the inevitable demands for emergency assistance or unscheduled visits. The managers became frustrated because they could never put their systems in place, and the workers and clients often felt out of control over their daily activity.

Surely the keeping of "records in shoe boxes," which occurred in the days before the state takeover of welfare, was no model. And no one in the 1980s can oppose making use of computers to record and track appropriate information. But many began to feel that the leadership—especially in EOHS, DPW, and DMH—became more interested in the record keeping than in the content of what was happening at the service workplace.[3] As one union official expressed the frustration: "They were like the librarian whose ideal library has all the books on the shelves with no one reading them. They wanted all the forms in order even if it meant we could not do our work."

Deinstitutionalization is another striking change since 1966. No one can deny that there were serious problems with the state hospitals for the mentally ill, state schools for the retarded, and state training schools for delinquents that defined the system then. The extent of the shift out of old institutions is still truly amazing and laudatory. Few clients or "outsiders" who ever visited the old, crowded, forbidding institutions will mourn their passing.

The question remains, however, whether the state has truly de-institutionalized or whether it only replaced large institutions with smaller ones.[4] There is still legitimate professional debate about the best form of care for the most troubled youth, the most disturbed mental patients, or most severely handicapped. Often this debate was squelched during the headlong push to deinstitu-tionalize, and the alternatives posed were extreme: we either "warehouse" such people or we provide open living. But, if the question of which care is best is still unanswered, then neither a pell-mell push to "finish" deinstitutionalization, nor an automatic, full, never-to-be-reopened decision to stop it, will provide an answer. We may have reached a stage that demands subtlety and complex analysis—a style usually out of harmony with the rules of the Circle Game.

Another dramatic change has been the change in role for the private sector. As we have discussed, "private" providers now deliver a high percentage of the state's direct social services. Medicaid has allowed private doctors and hospitals to have a more extensive role in the health care of the poor, and has helped to create a massive public/private system of chronic care. In 1966, private agencies were much less involved, and were viewed much more as independent agents and advocates. Now a new role and a new definition of relationships is required.

To be sure, public officials and private providers have been pondering these problems. The trouble arises from having created the public/private system of human services before anyone even began to consider them. In 1966 many of the issues for human service programs were posed as those of getting "do-nothing" public agencies to do something. Now we have lots of people doing lots of things, we are just not sure of (1) what they are doing; (2) why they are doing it; (3) if what they are doing is what we need; and (4) how we decide the answers to any of the above questions.

Other organizational changes not highlighted in the text have taken place in Massachusetts human services and these changes do create part of the overall sense that some things have improved. Here we just list a few that seem important:

—The enactment of Chapter 766 has allowed more children with special needs to attend public schools.
—The development of a spectrum of women's services—such as

battered women's programs, rape crisis centers and women's health services—has added a whole new area to the array of social services. Limited public funding has become available, with all its costs and benefits.

—Home Care Corporations and the Older Americans Act have increased services for the elderly and SSI has reduced the stigma of receiving old-age assistance.

Changes for workers and clients

It is more difficult to enumerate the changes for workers and clients because of the illusive nature of the changes. However, a few are tangible enough to warrant mention.

First, unionization came to most public service workers during this period. Some state employees had been unionized, without collective bargaining rights, in 1966, but most workers in local welfare offices, central offices, and clinics were not. Union organizing began in many places in the late sixties and by the early seventies had made such gains that the legislature agreed to permit collective bargaining and public-sector unions and formed an Alliance of state public employee unions in 1975. The election, then, brought unionization by fiat to many state employees—especially those outside the Greater Boston area. It also occurred at a time when the faltering economy meant an end to the great growth which had been a pattern for ten years. Many workers, therefore, became union members exactly when the unions were able to achieve the least gains for their membership.

These factors, plus some bitter infighting and/or charges of corruption within some unions, contributed to the weakness of the impact of unionization on the system. The continued existence of a civil service system has also confused the picture. Often it seemed as if neither administrators, workers, or union officials were quite sure what their respective roles were, especially around critical issues involving the quality of human service work. One union official put it this way:

We did not want to be a union which just counted caseload numbers. Many of us originally started as part of a client-oriented caucus and saw the union being in existence to provide better, more responsive service.

But it was hard, if not impossible, to do this. We *did* have to count caseload numbers and protect employees in a traditional way, before we could have any legitimacy with the membership. And with the new push for a "management approach" we often had to fight administrations over things which had been handled more informally in the past. But they couldn't seem really to figure out what to do with us either.

A mental health worker who was even more skeptical about the impact of unionization: "I used to be in the union. Now I'm on a grant and I'm not. It should make a difference, but it doesn't seem to matter at all." And, of course, the growth in contracted private agencies means that there are a whole new set of people providing "public" services who are not unionized and are in small agencies which are very difficult to organize.

For those who see unions as a basic protection for workers, such circumstances are not exciting. However, the upcoming crisis in human service budgets, with its accompanying layoffs, may revive a critical role for the unions. There has already been some indication that management may be able to use the "sanctity of collective bargaining agreements" as a way to stave off certain cuts. As one unionist commented recently: "I don't care what reasons they have, whether it's to protect their budgets or their salaries or their prestige or what. If they want to hide behind our union contract to fight cutbacks, more power to them."

Another, somewhat contradictory change during this period has been the concern with *professionalism* in the human service work force. In 1966, the social work professionals in DPW were primarily in the Division of Child Guardianship. Most welfare workers received on-the-job training but were not subject to rigid "professional" standards. Institutional workers in mental health and juvenile programs were often hired as much for their stamina as for their professional skills. The professional social work and medical schools, of course, prepared some students for work in the public sector but the prestige was low and such employees were not widely dispersed throughout the system.

The late sixties and early seventies brought an increase in both community paraprofessionals and better educated nonprofessionals into the field, especially in youth services, elderly services, and children's services. These people were often highly motivated and energetic workers, but they were not professionally trained to deal with some of the more difficult human problems. By 1976 a push was on for training, and, by implication, for more professionalism. There were calls to license social workers (and such legislation was passed in 1979). Many community mental health clinics began to seek "third-party payments" and to worry about the credentials of their employees, as did private agencies who sought contracts with the state. And the existence of extensive Title XX training programs, confused as the system for providing them was, also served to build an expectation that all levels of human service workers were expected to be professional. The culmination of this approach could be seen in the new Department of Social Services, which was widely hailed as a chance for a "professional approach" to child abuse.[5]

Perhaps ironically, given the above, the final change we see for Massachusetts human service workers was a *decline of job security*. In 1966 most public service workers were civil servants with what appeared to be lifelong job security. Indeed, a major barrier to deinstitutionalization was said to be the workers in the state institutions who "couldn't be fired." But, as grants and contracted services increased, a new group of workers began delivering services and experiencing a high degree of instability. Grants came and went, small contracted agencies faded or state priorities changed. And, by the end of this period, the insecurity began to be anticipated, if not experienced, by state workers.

Our interviews were conducted in 1979, with a few in 1980, so it is difficult to assess if public workers actually experienced great fears for their jobs in 1978, but surely by 1979 there was nervousness, and by 1980 there was real fear. One long-term mental health worker summarized the change well in the fall of 1980: "We were always safe. Our jobs might be hell but we had them if we could stand it. Deinstitutionalization was confusing and no one knew what would happen, but we thought, finally, we would be OK. But now, with the governor and all the talk about Proposition 2½, you have to worry about what's going to happen. Who knows?"

The changes for clients are even harder to analyze. Of course, we cannot deny that there were *more services* available. Medicaid made health care more accessible; the increase in social services made day care and other services available in greater number, and with less difficulty than in 1966. Food stamps became available. The growth of community mental health programs meant more options for people in stress. The increase in elderly programs and the availability of children's advocates from OFC meant that there were more places for a needy person to go to get services—the Welfare Department became less central. The institution of SSI meant that elderly and disabled poor were no longer welfare clients.

Such changes must matter, the facts are there. But no client we interviewed—or, for that matter, no worker—expressed more than a passing notice of the changes in service.[6] As we noticed the pattern, we began to ask directly about whether people felt there were more services. Most said they weren't sure, but one woman's response may help explain the problem:

Maybe there were more services. But I never noticed because I never had enough. It seems like I spent all my years on welfare just trying to survive. When something new came along I applied for it, but it was hard to get too excited because usually there were just more forms and another wait before you got half of what you needed. I do remember food stamps, though, because we got to stop getting that awful canned meat from surplus foods!

So, perhaps, we have hit on a special reason why it is so hard to escape the Circle Game. Because the benefits never are "enough," they seldom are appreciated, and may just serve to spur people on to want more. Like many forms of caring—as mothers so well know—the value, to the provider as well as the receiver and the society, may lie in the act of giving, not in any recognition or reward. Only when what is needed, or expected, is not there is concern and attention expressed.

Maybe this also helps explain why human service professionals and administrators have adopted a style of appeal that is negative: "We can't meet all these needs, please help us"; "We deserve a bigger budget in order to fulfill the unmet needs." In this way agencies can get some credit for trying—and failing—because there is so little recognition for what is accomplished. However, the outside world may not understand this device and may come, over time, to view human service agencies as always failing.

Social services came to be seen as a right during this period. In 1966, welfare advocacy groups had come to speak of "welfare rights," meaning rights to income maintenance. But services were seldom considered. Yet as poverty program services developed and as the women's movement began its push for day care and other services, this began to change. The growth in services funded by contracting, and the open public-planning process mandated by Title XX, together created a sense that services were a desirable good. Similar effects came from the increase in elderly services funded through OAA. (Indeed, a conservative criticism of the Department of Social Services was that it offered services as "entitlements.")

The end result of such developments was that, in their own lurching way, Massachusetts citizens were expanding their "bottom line" for what is expected of a decent society, and thereby creating a critical starting place for future struggles.

The scale and nature of client militance changed from 1966 to 1978. Welfare rights demonstrations set a tone for the sixties, even if they did not touch all clients' lives. Angry shouting, civil disobedience, and threatening slogans were the norm, and were a part of a larger social climate of protest and anger, especially among black people. Advocacy groups, like the Taskforce on Children Out of School and militant community groups, set a style of confrontation and anger that had important effects. In a short time most agencies revived sleepy advisory boards, or established new ones with "community participation." The rhetoric and the reality created a sense that people were fighting for their rights, and winning.

By the mid-seventies the tempo lessened, nationally and locally. Some groups continued and, as we have seen, fought against workfare or particular issues. But the overall sense of struggle declined, so it was hard to see any improvements. And, indeed, many agencies were relieved about the lessening of pressure; as one welfare official noted: "We didn't have to face the fires that Ott or Minter did. We could make needed changes without as much outside pressure."

Throughout the seventies, organizers and recipients kept searching for sparks to relight the fire without ever knowing where or when they would appear. And now, in the eighties, when they seem to be rekindling, activists still must face the questions of how to frame a welfare rights movement without the supporting atmosphere of a general social climate of militancy.

And Some Stay the Same

Many of the unchanging aspects of human services are intangible. People have a sense of déjà vu. Perhaps part of the reason is that even as program content and mandates shift, the same issues re-emerge. In 1978, as in 1966, administrators were concerned about accountability, about costs, about the legislature, about some unforeseen disaster making the front pages. Workers were aware of impossible responsibilities, frustrations, and how hierarchical structures make it impossible to function.[7]

And clients felt poor. In 1980, 596,000 people could be defined as poor. In 1966 the best estimates are that more than 440,000 people were poor. Although it cannot be denied that Medicaid, food stamps, and the availability of wider services improved the lot of poor people, it also cannot be denied that the people using almost all the services here have reasons to feel poor. For one, they still are poor, by definition. For another, the very act of using these services is seen as an affirmation of one's poverty.

Recently, conservative theorists have taken to insisting that poverty has disappeared in America, because all of the social programs have eliminated it.[8] There are many ways to dispute this argument, which is often semantic and more political than economic. Here we can only counter with a quote from one of the women we met later than others in this study, a young black female college student with only one child who is on welfare and who receives Medicaid, food stamps, and Title XX day care. Because of all of these "in-kind" benefits many analysts would see her as having risen out of poverty, as being an example of a "change" since 1966. Her reply, given in the fall of 1981, was telling:

What do they mean, I'm not poor? What is poor if it's not having people in grocery lines comment on what you buy with your food stamps? What is poor if it's not staying home all weekend before the check comes, because you don't even have car fare? Or that you have to switch dentists for your child because the dentist doesn't want to take Medicaid any more?
I'm poor because every time I see my welfare worker he tells me I'm poor. I'm poor because now they say I can't even go to school any more, that I have to take any job I can find even if it has no future, no hope.
   It doesn't matter that maybe I get a little more now than I might have gotten ten years ago. I'm still poor and they won't let me forget it!

Finally, what stayed the same is the pessimism of people in the system. The National Study Service report noted that workers and administrators were often demoralized and doubtful that anything could change for the better and that clients expected to be shuffled around, disrespected, and frustrated. In 1978, we found all of the same sentiments. Burnout was an expected state for workers. Even administrators acknowledged that "morale" was a problem. About client concerns we found a stone wall of hopelessness, except from a few organizers. Everyone else we interviewed felt that "the price of being on welfare is being shuffled around by the bureaucracy," or that public-service clients "just have to put up with a lot, what can you do?" Only the most active saw reasons to expect change. And even they were often nagged by doubts: "Everybody feels hopeless, and that's what makes it hopeless. We have to keep fighting for ourselves, though, even if we're not sure how to win. There is nothing else to do."

National Perspectives

Sometimes, to get perspective, it helps to see that Massachusetts was not alone in all the frustration, pain, and unpraised changes. There have been few similar studies of other states, but there is enough information to allow us to remember that not all the problems were our fault.[9] Before trying to evaluate the meaning and implications of the Circle Game it may be useful to consider such national patterns.

First, we must not forget that changes in the national economy created similar options and strains across the nation.[10] The sixties were boom times with low unemployment, high economic growth, and a spirit of fiscal buoyancy, fueled by spending for the Vietnam War. In Congress new programs were passed, costing large amounts of money, without more than normal complaints about expenditures. The Johnson administration pushed for and got domestic programs of a social magnitude unknown since the New Deal. (Indeed, some commentators first thought that Reagan only wanted to wipe away these programs, not the more basic benefits that have since come under attack.) Medicaid was ultimately the most expensive of these programs, and its influence in creating an atmosphere of "runaway costs" in social welfare cannot be underestimated. Nationally, Medicaid costs went from $1.367 billion in the first year of implementation to 5.213 billion in 1970 and by 1975 they had risen to 12.968 billion. These were whopping expenditures provided with no ceiling, and they went directly to doctors, hospitals, nursing homes, and pharmacists who were more-successful then poor people at heading off opposition to "their" program.[11] Although all states did not initially participate as fully in Medicaid as Massachusetts—few had as powerful a medical establishment—all experienced similar patterns of growth.

Medicaid costs are central to the story of costs "skyrocketing" but they seldom make the media as a major source of the "welfare mess." In Washington as in Massachusetts, it is easier to attack women on welfare than to attack doctors. Yet, nationally, the pattern reproduces that of Massachusetts; Medicaid costs exceed those of AFDC by 40 percent. What is even more interesting, and seldom discussed, is that Medicaid goes disproportionately to the elderly and disabled. Although 70 percent of all those eligible for Medicaid are women and children on AFDC, they only account for 30 percent of the costs. The rest go to the elderly and disabled. This is true in Massachusetts and nationally.[12] The point is *not* to suggest that elderly and disabled people do not deserve Medicaid. Rather it is to show that, nationally and in Massachusetts, something funny is going on. Welfare recipients are blamed for becoming unmotivated and dependent on a system where over half of the costs are medical. Since no one seems to suggest that it is access to "free" medical care which makes people dependent, we might argue that poor people in Massachusetts and across the nation are being asked to tighten their belts because medical costs are so high.

Similarly, federal patterns help us understand Massachusetts's problems with social services. After 1967, amendments to the Social Security Act allowed states to purchase services from private agencies—at little cost to the states because the agencies donated the 25 percent matching funds—several states ran amuck.[13] In California, New York, and Illinois, especially, state administrators began to purchase all kinds of services, with little or no planning. Massachusetts tried to get on the bandwagon but was never really committed to such large-scale spending. However, because of the actions of these states, and to head off "uncontrollable" costs, a federal cap was placed on social service spending in 1972. So, by the time Massachusetts wanted to expand its social services commitment, its money was limited.

To make matters worse, the language and public approach of Title XX, implemented in 1975, forced the Welfare Department into a position of seeming to promise a new involvement to private agencies and less-poor citizens, while it offered them no more money to spend. Like most other states, Massachusetts officials were not really even aware of the double bind they were in until it was too late to stop the demands for increased expenditures, the new bureaucratic procedures, and the sense that, once again, "false promises" had been made.

Finally, it would be unfair to Massachusetts officials not to acknowledge the contradictory role of federal initiatives around reorganization.[14] Throughout the Nixon/Ford administration, and to some extent into the Carter administration, federal planners were seized with the idea that services integration, coordination, and redesign could improve the duplication and waste of service delivery. They offered the lure of "capacity-building" grants to help, as well as the chance to attend lots of conferences to discuss one's program. All over the country, not just in Massachusetts, frustrated administrators went along—to the glee of thousands of planners, organizational consultants, and graduate-student researchers.[15]

However, there was a catch to all this redesign; at best, it took place only with "seed money" from the feds. But worse, all the training, pamphlets, and systems-design workshops didn't consider political realities, labor issues, and the intractability of human service needs. So, even though some efforts to integrate services were somewhat effective as organizational tools, few could withstand the political pressures that arose as failing economies demanded cuts, as agencies retreated into turf battles, and as clients—whether they had a human service generalist or an old-fashioned social worker—still felt pain.

The result was that many administrators came away feeling foolish and discredited. One veteran of Area Strategy, Massachusetts's large-scale version of this approach, could come away feeling

burned, burned, burned. It sounded like an OK idea. I thought everyone up above really meant to follow through this time. So I pulled out all the stops, I sponsored talks to my staff and really pushed this thing. We sent people to meetings and hearings. And then, poof. The secretary is gone. The head of the thing is in trouble because he's been too much of a bastard. It's all gone and I'm left feeling like a fool. It will be a long time before I go along with anything like *that* again.

Similar stories may soon be told about deinstitutionalization, another state effort which is duplicated elsewhere. The point here is not to pass the blame, but to suggest that we had best not forget that the Circle Game is national too, and that the way it is played in Washington both mirrors and controls the way it is played in Massachusetts.

The Meaning of the Circle Game

The Circle Game is a metaphor for how society, organizations, administrators, workers, and clients interact and cope with situations where it is very difficult, if not impossible, to win. To win would mean to accomplish humanitarian, caring goals, to be rewarded, and then to move on to higher goals. Such options are available to no one in the system. The tragedy is that most cannot see this, so the energy that does exist is spent in blaming or passing the buck, in denial, or in angry, barely repressed hostility.

It all begins because of a false premise—that the existing economic and social order can provide adequate, humane care for those in need if only the organizations are efficient enough, the managers smart enough, the workers diligent enough, and the clients motivated enough. Large-scale ideological means (like schools, the media, the American creed) are used to convince us all that this premise is true. And most people, at all social levels, believe it to be.[16] So the game begins and everyone plays his or her unhappy role.

The general public and their elected representatives want to see themselves as creating a humane, caring society, especially in a place with the history and concentrated intelligence of Massachusetts. So laws are passed with flowery language that promises much too much. When a flood occurs in Italy or one fireman needs a heart operation, the coffers open. The outpouring is real, heart felt, and occurs only once.

The legislature passes Medicaid with all options and pats itself on the back because "Massachusetts will have the best." But two years later no one wants to hear about costs that double every year. Governors institute massive reorganization plans with a call for modernized state government, but abandon them mid-stream when the economy and election pressures make them a liability. Their cabinet secretaries then have only their personal and symbolic power for accomplishing anything, in an arena where too much personal exposure marks a person for downfall. Recipients are piously urged to live within their means, when their only "fraud" is a secret selling job to earn Christmas money, but millions of dollars are spent year after year on computer systems that never work. Governors and the legislature fight and workers' paychecks and clients' subsistence checks are held up—but the fight is over "important principles." The public is outraged that someone could throw a child out in the garbage, but do not want to pay for open-ended day care programs that might take the pressure off violent families.

In the face of the contradictions of a society that wants to be generous but doesn't want anyone to dare to demand generosity, or to need it too often, administrators try to build programs. They have many people to please. First, there is a legislature that wants no scandals, no cost overruns, only show-case programs, grand promises, and self-flagellation over problems—as well as, perhaps, a job for the son of a worthy constituent. Then there is a governor who wants peace, satisfied legislators, and heart-rending programs to visit, so he can have pictures taken, and promise a "new commitment." Third, there are the other administrators at equal levels with whom one must shine, but not too brightly, lest one be seen as a threat. The adept administrator must be cooperative, but not too cooperative, because that would be a sign of weakness, a sign that another agency could move into one's turf. Finally, with everyone, one must *be careful* neither to expose too much about one's problems nor to commit too much to a risky innovation, in case it might be too identified with the agency if it fails.

It is no wonder that, in the face of such stresses, few administrators develop mutually supportive management teams. It is safer to keep secrets from even central staff, because of the fear of leaks. It makes sense to shift someone who is good at one job to "save" another program, even if the issues are totally different and the person liked what she or he was doing originally. Ultimately, it is only natural that real substantive discussions of policy issues, and their effects on clients and workers, never occur because there is never time, but also because they might expose differences or ignorances that are best left buried.

The end result is administrators who must over-promise and keep secrets, who must blame ill-trained workers for failures or clients who have been "too demoralized to achieve." Being "realistic" will mean obfuscation and downplaying the lessons of one's expertise. Even when innovations do occur that bring real—if slow —change for the better, there can be little honest pride, because successes must be exaggerated and the continuing problems— which could serve as a direction for future plans—must be covered up. Finally, the goal of real leadership, not "management," seems lost because it threatens everyone else in the system and implies that one is willing to fight too hard, become too passionate, and care too much.

Workers, too, are trapped by being held accountable when they are not, by being tied down by rules that make no sense, by being forced to push clients out so they have a manageable caseload, by all the cycles that have been mentioned here and that are analyzed so thoroughly in Michael Lipsky's book, *Street-level Bureaucracy*.[17] Saddest are the ways people are forced to defend themselves at the cost of respect and concern for clients. One man on our research team had to quit his job because, "I was starting to hate people for wanting things, for coming to us with the same stories when we couldn't really help." Others stay and clients know they are hated.

Private providers are caught too. Many local program directors have gone to several agencies for contracts, to be "diversified." But they face complicated consequences in resource fights. Neither public nor fully private, they may not know whom to defend or oppose, as one provider, with a medieval cast of mind, remarked:

It will be like the War of the Roses. We could face a situation where everybody is related to someone else through contract and when we try to fight another agency we come to find out that we need their approval for another contract. There will be cousins and brothers and sisters on different sides of the battles on different days. No one will know what is happening and no one will know how to declare the war over or lost because they won't know who is on which side.

And, of course, the clients are left with few options but to dislike everyone and believe no one. They have already been used as shock troops when small agencies wanted to fight but were afraid to do it themselves. They have been put on boards and been ignored or patronized. They have heard all their pathologies described and used to explain why nothing can ever change. And they have been offered self help programs when agencies could think of nothing else to do.

Finally, then, the game nobody can win is lost because nobody can trust. With the 1970s we saw a growing interdependency among agencies and a decreasing level of trust—for reasons that were very real. Contracted agencies couldn't trust their contractor or other competing agencies. State agencies had to compete with each other. Legislators came to see everyone as hopeless beggars, even as they made everyone beg in order to get anything. Agencies and client groups viewed the legislators, or the governor or the top administrators (pick your target and your issue) as social Neanderthals. Contracting agencies could not trust the agencies they gave money to nor did they have the capacity to monitor agencies to discover if what they most feared was happening. The feds didn't believe anybody and nobody believed them. State workers' unions jockeyed for position within their shaky Alliance. Workers feared client fraud or "acting out" would get them in trouble. Client groups fought each other for crumbs. Individual clients feared harassment in order to fill some workers' "redetermination" quotas. Workers in contracted agencies never knew whether to blame their boss or the funding agency for their problems. And clients of these agencies never knew whether to blame the workers, the bosses, or the funding agency.

Each actor within this sad scenario had good reasons to distrust everyone else. But the end result was that our circle became a knot strangling everyone in an irredeemable stalemate.

If any change in the dynamic is to take place in the next few years, some trust must be established somewhere. Today the New Right has rejected the premise that began the Circle Game and is arguing out loud that since we can't do everything we should do nothing, or next to nothing. In the face of such an attack, perhaps some new alliances can be built, based on a common goal of doing the best we can. Perhaps administrators could become brave enough to defend their clients and their workers, or be replaced if they will not. Legislators might stop demanding lies one week and confessions the next. Clients of different agencies might be able to create new coalitions. We are not naive enough to suggest an idealistic "kiss and make up" strategy but we are fed up enough with the incredible waste of human energy to suggest that somebody do something, and that requires somebody trusting somebody else. Like it or not.

Winners and Losers

Before going on to the implications for the 1980s, we cannot resist ending our review by giving awards to the winners and losers for the period from 1966 to 1978. In order to be fair, we have divided our awards into three categories: the organizational category, the policy category, and the human-impact category. As the envelopes are brought forward we should note that the criteria for selection were impressionistic and based as much on public image as on available evidence. In this we consider our judges to be highly in tune with their audience. We also want to remind our readers that winning for a past period may not be a good predictor of future success. Indeed, our audience is fickle; so this decade's Big Winner may be the next's Big Loser.

Now, the first prize in the organizational category was—the Department of Mental Health. As it deinstitutionalized it nicely avoided the overly pure devotion to deinstitutionalization that had been the political downfall of Jerry Miller and DYS. DMH also kept the legitimacy that derives from direct-service delivery (and lots of psychiatrists), which both DEA and OFC lacked.

The private providers were second-place winners, although the limits imposed by a contradictory role, inflation, and bureaucratic red tape began to lessen their increase in stature by the end of the period.

The Executive Office of Human Services endured, which must be seen as worthy of an honorable mention. It also helped to support a closer knitting together of state agencies (some call it the Solid Front) at the top levels.

The Welfare Department lost points by converging, then gained some again by diverging. The aftermath of the state takeover was a bureaucratic nightmare, but the agency began to regain its institutional identity again by sending its old and disabled clients to Social Security and its social services to DSS.

The Department of Elder Affairs won awards as a best supporting actor and the Office for Children was a crowd pleaser but could never convince the judges which category to place it in.

In the policy category we again give DMH star billing. Once the deinstitutionalization policy was determined, the department never wavered, despite worker and public doubts and the complexity of actual implementation. The numbers don't lie.

A close runner-up in this category is Jerald Stevens and his management approach, especially within the Welfare Department. Here again, we cannot fail to recognize steadfastness of purpose regardless of the consequences.

In the policy category there are few other contenders because most agencies spent this time reacting ad hoc to crises instead of formulating or implementing clear policy. DYS might be recognized here except that it seemed to lose the courage of its convictions toward the end. The Welfare Department deserves a special award for remaining unaware of instituting significant policy. With Medicaid and Title XX purchases it became the ultimate provider for great amounts of services and seemed only to be realizing what it had done by the time the award period was coming to a close.

Again OFC waffled and DEA was more concerned with coordinating than formulating policy. In past years private providers excelled in this category but during the period under review they were too busy writing grant proposals to qualify.

No awards were given in the human-impact category. The judges decided that because this factor had not been considered in planning or implementing the programs under review, it would be unfair to consider it as a criterion for evaluation.

How's that for a Circle Game?

8 Will the Circle Be Unbroken?

This study began with some doubts about how a history of human services programs which ended with 1978 could be relevant to the 1980s. Surely none of the actors in our Circle Game had to respond to budget cuts of the magnitude imposed by Proposition 2½ and Reaganism. Nor did they face the ideological attack against the goals, as well as the practice, of human services that has been launched by the New Right. All were dealing more with the consequences of growth and the need for bureaucratic containment of expansion than they were with radical efforts to stop, or fundamentally alter, the process of human service activity. Such dramatic shifts make it understandable for critics to suggest that the Circle Game is an outdated critique, a set of dynamics and expectations totally unrelated to the present environment.

However, our analysis of the period from 1966 to 1978 suggests a different, two-fold response. First, we must acknowledge that the criticisms of Ronald Reagan, and of his less folksy allies, are partially based on a recognition of the same failures and contradictions within the human service system that we have found. Like it or not, the stories Candidate Reagan kept on his notecards regarding government ineptitude, confusion, and curious judgments could all have been true in Massachusetts. Similarly, we cannot deny that Proposition 2½ appealed to legitimate frustrations with the Circle Game. We need, then, to analyze the problems, to understand how they contributed to the criticisms, and to offer counter solutions to those posed by the Right.

Second, our analysis also shows that, despite all the failures and absurdities of the system, it does harbor many decent people who are struggling bravely to uphold the public's responsibility to provide care for its citizens. They are often thwarted and frustrated, but they have made some important—if seldom recognized—

gains. We owe it to these advocates and workers to fight to retain their accomplishments, not to allow blanket criticisms of the system's failures to undo its successes.

We cannot just relegate the past to some dusty nostalgia album, in an amoral historical equivalent of zero-based budgeting. Instead we need to retrieve and celebrate the successes, as well as remember and overcome the failures, if we are to find a positive base from which to propose a different future for the 1980s.

Lessons from the Past

As we have seen, it is easier to find the negative lessons of the Circle Game than to discover the positive ones. The problems are so obvious that a high-level DMH official, hoping for the commissioner's job, could tell a public gathering that "the past ten years have proved that the public sector cannot provide services." The system has, in many ways, discredited itself and it takes but a minute to review the reasons why.

First, there were false promises made to the public, the workers, and the clients, albeit because they were what many wanted to hear. The period began with promises about community mental health, unlimited Medicaid benefits, the benefits of state control of welfare. In between substantial promises were made about the results of deinstitutionalization, computerization, about centralization one year and decentralization the next. The epoch ended with inevitably unreachable claims for new computer matches to end fraud and for the ability of skilled professionals to cure child abuse.

At last all these promises came due. Some people—especially those who never wanted them met in the first place—remembered and, when the time was right, reminded everyone else of how much was promised and how little achieved.

Second, failures were annually used to justify needed policies and expenditures. It was the failures of state institutions that led to deinstitutionalization, the failures of local welfare that justified a state takeover, the failures of some state agencies to deal with children that justified another agency to advocate for them. Money was needed for computers because workers made errors. Private services were purchased because they were better than public ones, although we soon found that their staff desperately needed training too. Every innovation seemed to come with an indictment of past mistakes, along with over-promises for the future. It is no wonder that people finally started to question the wisdom of funding this year's solution only to have it become next year's problem.

Third, neither the imposition of an umbrella agency nor other efforts to coordinate and integrate services seemed able to stop the bureaucratic infighting. Workers found themselves unable to talk to each other and clients remained uncertain about where to go, even as administrators jockeyed to stay in control of efforts to avoid duplications. Outsiders and insiders could look at all this and begin to despair for the possibilities of change.

Fourth, the benefits of professional expertise became confused. At first paraprofessionals and community workers were praised and hired precisely because they lacked professional distance. Later, the call was for more training and professionalism for everyone. Yet, at the same time, agencies were increasingly run—and policies defined—by individuals whose expertise had little to do with the skills needed to deliver services. So we arrived at a place where no one's knowledge was legitimate, where few could achieve widespread support as representing the needs of the system.

Fifth, the real benefits that were developed or fought for during the period were often presented as going only to a particularly needy group, not as desirable commodities that improved the lives of all. SSI was implemented as a bureaucratic shift in how old and disabled people received their checks, instead of as a substantial shift in public responsibility for a group who otherwise made greater—and increasingly unmeetable—demands on their families. Food stamps were presented as special supplements to the most poor, rather than as a basic preventive public health initiative to improve the general level of nutrition in the society. Granted, it might have been hard to convince a wider public of such general benefits, but the effort was not made in this way—regardless of the dominant mode of over promising. (We see how Head Start, a national program, somehow made this argument and has now become a protected program.)

And finally, as we said in chapter 2, all of these and other problems were exaggerated by the inability of the professional leadership to admit to the impossibility—in this society at least—of solving any of the basic social problems that their programs addressed. So, what could be done was not valued because what could not was never acknowledged.

It is less easy to enumerate the positive lessons from the Circle Game. They occurred less systematically and are more subject to question, but they do exist and need to be recognized.

First, as we argued in the last chapter, change and improvement did occur, even if neither as smoothly nor as fully as they were planned. The closing of prisons for young people was such a change, as was the creation of a variety of programs for the mentally ill and retarded. Similarly, the creation of one uniform welfare system was an advancement over the disparities that existed before 1966. OFC and DEA did offer clients a place to go, even as they could not meet all their needs. In short, the reason for exposing the problems with all these programs is so that they are more able to do the good they are capable of, not to destroy them completely.

Second, people have proven that they can organize and fight to achieve more of their needs. Welfare rights groups did this; parents of the retarded and handicapped people learned the same lesson. Legal service attorneys learned the limits that can be placed on insensitive agencies, even in times of cuts. In short, by looking at the history we can see that advocacy can and did make a difference. Admittedly, the circumstances that yield effective organizing are not obvious, nor easily reproducible, but this does not discredit the power of militance when it can be mobilized.

Third, as we have seen, by a range of conscious and not so conscious means, citizens have been able to expand the definitions of what is theirs by rights. Women and minorities struggled to demand whole new categories of services, as have handicapped people. The work of professional and community activists—and of dedicated professionals and workers who built on their demands —have helped to create a sense that services, as well as basic subsistence, are ours by right when we need them. In 1978, the demand for continued and increased support for day care, children's programs and elderly services was taken for granted by large numbers of the poor and not-so-poor. It is exactly this sense that "entitlements" have been expanded that so infuriates the Right, because of their expansive economic and social effects. Here, from our perspective, we can be proud of such an increased social vision and fight for it as a major achievement of the period under review.

Finally, the ability of individuals—like so many of the workers, clients, and administrators interviewed here—to keep their integrity and dedication alive, in the face of the system failures offers a fundamental positive lesson. These people, who know the problems with the Circle Game so much more intimately than any outsider can, did not quit. Instead, they kept finding one more loophole for developing a creative program and providing needed services, or one more way to keep going despite the efforts to beat them down. If they can keep at it, so must we, because their work confirms our initial assumption, that the existence of a public system of human services is a vital and sustaining social good, one that is essential to achieving a caring society.

Unacceptable Responses

Three different contemporary responses are proposed for the 1980s which draw their own lessons from the Circle Game. All contain serious flaws that must be understood, at least in brief, in order to formulate a response with any hope of building on the strengths and changing the weaknesses in the current system.

The New Right is most important both nationally and through its Massachusetts organization, Citizens for Limited Taxation. These people vary along the spectrum of opinions regarding human services. At the least, all agree that the Circle Game is doomed, that public service programs cannot help being bad because they are costly, redundant, create dependence, and are usually unnecessary. The minimal demand is that disorganized and inefficient programs be streamlined, made more accountable to local priorities, and only allowed to provide benefits for the "truly needy." The hard core would question the assumptions built into the Social Security Act itself. They represent the successors to groups who fought all New Deal programs, who view social planning and social work as "socialism," and who see individual "freedom" as the highest ideological goal. For these people budget cuts are only a means to a deeper end—the elimination of almost all public programs, even public schools.[1]

The New Right arguments are based on three major premises about the Circle Game. First, they argue that past benefits have eliminated most poverty in this country and have undermined the work ethic and the ability of United States industry to compete in the international markets.[2] Because of over-generous programs we hurt all workers and created an "underclass" of people who are dependent on the state for generations without motivation to go to work. The solution demanded is simple: public handouts should be eliminated or made so degrading and punitive that only those with no other options for survival will apply.

Second, the rise of feminism and the consequent decline of the family through a new morality are seen as supported by human service programs.[3] Women will no longer stay home and take care of their children, husbands, and needy relatives because they have options created by feminist demands. Therefore, in order to restore the independence and primacy of the family—and of true womanhood—program options must be eliminated as desirable choices for most women.

Finally, the growth of government to supply these debilitating programs is seen as weakening the basic fiber of American society.[4] Even businessmen have become too dependent on the state, while at the same time their initiative is sapped by government regulations. Here there is disagreement. Some want the military arm of the state strengthened, which is viewed as possible only with reduced regulations and reduced domestic spending. Others see the growth of the state in all its parts as dangerous and are less interested in maintaining military spending. But all agree on the harm that federal social programs can do to the American character.

Much more could be said about the New Right, and about its internal contradictions. What is most important here is to recognize that polls suggest that this hard-core analysis is not the source of the widespread appeal of Reagan or other New Right politicians and policies.[5] Such views are not often stated baldly. Instead, New Right leaders allow the Circle Game to speak for them. They campaign against government waste and inefficiency, and simply for an end to government programs that have "proved they cannot succeed." Seldom, and only to select audiences, do they mention their opposition to all programs, especially to those that might have a chance for success.

Our other two groups of unacceptable respondents are neither so organized nor so ideological. Instead, they represent two strains of reactions to the New Right. First, there are what can be called the "New Realists." [6] These are upper-level human service professionals in the public sector, although there are many from private agencies in this group also. They offer a professional cover to the New Right, by proposing to do the cuts themselves. They too acknowledge the failures of public human services and admit that a "realistic assessment" confirms that the public sector cannot provide services. They are willing to retreat from deinstitutionalization, from the expansion of rights, and from any fights for expanded services because of the unsuccessful past records of service providers. Their reward for such a role is that they stay—or gain —in power and have authority over whatever is left after the cutting is done.[7]

The New Realists make a slightly different offer to workers, clients, and advocates within the system. Here, they often claim to oppose the cuts and the new philosophy but argue that it is better that they make the cuts rather than having someone who does not know the system allowed to do it. Pleas for opposition are dismissed as "unrealistic" and naive, "in these times." There is an implied threat that, if they are not successful at implementing cuts, the New Right will move in and things will be even worse. Already, the New Realists are finding academic counterparts in university-research programs, where people who once studied how to decentralize service systems in order to make them more responsible to the community are now quite willing to take money to develop information systems for workfare programs.

Finally, there is a dwindling, but still prestigious, "this too will pass" school. These people are most often liberal professionals not as directly involved with human service delivery as the New Realists. They tend to be more defensive about existing programs and less willing to acknowledge that the Circle Game ever existed. Their argument is that it is the wrong time to be critical of human service programs. For them, discussion of past failures implies disloyalty and aid to the enemy. Their response is usually one of suggesting publicity campaigns conducted by posters and flyers showing sad, spindly-legged children who are in need of help from our dedicated social service professionals. They are vocal and moving in their appeals for social justice, but are often as unwilling to be openly hostile to the New Realists or the New Right as they are to consider new alternatives.

The passing of time may drive many of this inclination into the camp of the New Realists, out of a hope to influence them, or to keep options open. Many seem to be turning to private practice and health care in efforts to wait out the current storm and in the hope that, some day, things will be better, "as the pendulum swings back our way again."

Of course, this last group is more attractive than the first two. But they avoid any sense of responsibility for a system that seems to justify the current crisis. In the end, their sense of privilege is an inadequate response to a situation where those less fortunate are losing their jobs and their careers, or their meager hopes for a life with dignity.

Denying the Circle Game exists, then, is as unacceptable a strategy as accepting it as a hopeless given. All three approaches leave clients vulnerable. Workers either lose their jobs or their ability to perform helpful—rather than hurtful—services. And the public is left by all "solutions" with reduced social expectations and diminished hope for the future.

Why It Is Hard to Fight

The basic assumption of this study is that any hope for change in the Circle Game, and a strong front against the New Right, depends on a recognition of the limitations of past programs and an attempt to build a positive strategy out of that critique. Yet this is, obviously, more easily said than done. We have developed bad habits and limited visions. As times get worse, and the criticisms more dangerous, it becomes even harder to escape from the daily pressures long enough to imagine alternatives, much less to fight to achieve them.

Perhaps the saddest way the system has weakened those who would change it is by dividing them from each other. The public that does not receive services has little identification with those who do. Workers and clients, particularly, have been pitted against each other in real battles for power. Clients are not, easily, going to stand up out of their foxholes and wave a peace sign to workers who have been forced to shoot at them for years, even if clients have developed a political analysis that suggests such a strategy. One organizer told a story which epitomizes the problem:

Last summer on Cape Cod something happened which makes me hesitate to build alliances with workers, no matter how "correct" that strategy is. We were fighting for summer housing, always a problem on the Cape. While we were outside demonstrating, welfare workers were ordered to guard the doors against us. They did. A scuffle occurred and there was fighting between some welfare social workers and some clients. So the next thing we know we were all in court charging each other with assault. How's that for class solidarity?

Similarly, workers are not sure how to work with clients. As one union leader noted: "It will be hard. Most workers have spent a lot of years thinking their clients were either sick, incapable of taking care of themselves, or deadbeats. That won't change easily." And the ways in which some workers view client demands continue to reflect the enduring class antagonisms experienced by one woman on our research team:

I couldn't understand why my WIN worker was so hostile. She kept being negative whenever I said that I wanted to find a job in human services, like I was trained for.
Finally, one day she came out and said it. She asked me, "who did I think I was, expecting a job for more money than she was making?"

There are other barriers to developing a base and a strategy for the 1980s. As we have seen, workers from different agencies and at different levels have been isolated from each other, and have learned distrust. Especially as job cuts are implemented, it may be difficult to find the unity that will be vital to any alternative approaches. And, it is also unclear what grounds exist for concerted approach between administrators and workers. Full-scale public attacks on social programs rarely differentiate between management and labor, so there would seem to be a chance for some unity in defense of desired programs. However, one union official is doubtful.

There are some people in management who really should be in the union. They don't really make policy or hire and fire people, they just do many bureaucratic tasks. We might be able to work with them. The people at the very top, though, seem to be out for themselves and their careers. They will do whatever they have to do to keep their place. Besides they have been blaming us for all the troubles in the department for years, why should they change?

On the other hand, many workers and mid-level administrators seem doubtful about the value of the unions in times of crisis. As one worker said:

I'm not sure I expect much help from the union. They have never been very effective at changing policy or at offering alternative ways to think about service work. They only seem able to think in terms of narrow issues, like seniority or caseload size.

And a mid-level administrator also seemed discouraged about possibilities for unity:

What really has to happen is that somebody needs to admit that, in many ways, we are all on the same side in this. I know it all sounds naive—and may not be true at the very top—but for now it is the integrity of all our work that is being threatened. I'm tired of being labeled "management" because I do paperwork in a central office. It doesn't mean I don't care about the work people do, or what happens to clients. And I want to get together with similar people in the department and try to figure out what to do, regardless of whether people are in the union or not.

Another problem facing human service workers and clients in the turmoil of the eighties is likely to be their own mental health. As we have seen, both groups have never had easy roles to play and during a time of diminishing public respect and slashed budgets this fact is bound to have its personal costs. The Policy Training Center, a Boston-based organization with a federal grant to help human service workers cope with the personal and social stresses of the "crisis," has faced an increasingly hard task. Many workers seemed too depressed and overwhelmed even to cope with "stress workshops," and courses that address broader political issues have been even less successful.[8] For clients the pressures are even worse, although many may have more experience dealing with uncertainty. As one woman put it, in the fall of 1981:

I feel like someone has torn all the parts of my life into little pieces and thrown them all up into the air. I don't know what to do because nothing is decided. I don't know whether they are going to make me leave school and go to work, whether my financial aid will still be there, whether my mother's minimal Social Security check will still come, and whether they will end my housing program. It's hard to know what to do first, since anything could happen.

Many workers find that their professional training has ill equipped them for considering alternatives, at a time when there is so much uncertainty. One high-level professional put it this way:

I was trained to be a planner. I still think that if I know enough information I can figure out options, at least. Even if politics caused the final decisions I could speculate about the choices. And it more or less worked, as bad as things have been. Now (summer 1981) I realize that nobody knows anything. They fight about state budgets due to Proposition 2½ and none of the old rules apply. And even when we get a budget we still wait to hear what will happen in Washington. Everyone is afraid to move.

Another aspect of the tension is the fear that many experience when they come to understand that information and good logic no longer win any arguments. The same planner commented: "I was an information junkie. I wanted to know everything because I thought it would help me convince people of what to do. Now I realize that nobody listens to me, no matter how good my information."

We might argue that such professionals are only coming to recognize what has always been true, that they too are workers within a system that affords them very little power. But, whatever the underlying reality, it is clear that such tensions make it more difficult for professional workers to think of new options in times of crisis.

Finally, even those most ready to consider plans and options for change—progressive human service activists—often find themselves weakened by internal confusions around two critical concerns: the family and the state.

Since the 1960s, many activists—including this author—moved from the New Left into women's and community work without fully understanding the complexity of our activity. We argued that women had rights to jobs, to sexual freedom, to single parenthood at the same time that we tried to support women's choices within the family. Now we find ourselves facing a simultaneous attack on poor women's rights to remain full-time mothers and on middle-class women's freedom to limit their caretaking roles within the family.[9]

It is easy to become confused under such assaults. We need to oppose "profamily" arguments that define the family as a holy unit, inevitably dependent on the mother to take care of everyone else. Yet we also must insist that women have rights to define their "work" as in the home and to demand public support for that work instead of being forced into unwanted "second jobs" outside the home. Human services must be defended, indeed, as mechanisms that *do* allow women to leave unhappy homes or to work outside the home and shift the patterns of dependency from private caretaking to public resources. At the same time, the use of "support services" to *force* women out of the home must be opposed. In the face of such tricky logic it is not surprising that many activists are immobilized.

Even more basic is the confusion we face regarding our expectations of the government. Throughout the period under review, many activists worked in public human service programs, or organized to demand better services, while maintaining an analysis that was highly skeptical of the ability of the capitalist state to do anything but oppress people.[10] We pushed for public services as a right, as a reformist demand, but we never seriously resolved the "contradiction" of what the capitalist welfare state was all about. During times of growth, or even level funding, the theoretical tension was not crucial. Activists could demand more services while fighting the agency that funded them. Indeed, we saw an entire state agency, the OFC, set up by the government to fight other agencies—almost as a "counter institution" within the bureaucracy.

Now such anomalous activities are more difficult to maintain, at least without clearer thought. As the pressure mounts to discredit the public sector and turn its functions over to private programs we must fight to maintain public responsibility. But we must also continue our criticisms of the overwhelming dangers stemming from large public bureaucracies. Progressives, more than anyone, have an analysis that explains the Circle Game as a function of the broader political and economic system. We understand how it helps to keep people from rebelling—or from dying and causing others to rebel; how it socializes people to accept the existing order; and how it preserves the status and income of certain classes. Yet our analysis also shows the importance of an ongoing quest for expanding social rights and benefits and the need to consistently demand more from the existing order. In times like these it is especially difficult to reconcile the two levels of analysis.[11]

In short, would-be leaders of efforts to break out of the Circle Game are caught in our own ideological dilemmas. Now, more than ever, the complexities of our analysis are baffling, just as we feel the greatest need for clarity. It is hard, then, not to confuse ourselves and anyone we try to work with in these critical times.

What Can Be Done?

Given all the above, it seems presumptuous to suggest actions. Yet we cannot forget one of our early interviewees who kept saying, "make it mean something. Don't just talk about all that without making it mean something." So we will conclude with some suggestions about how to make our case, about the positions that, taken together, may help to create a better version of the Circle Game.

As we were finishing this study a new understanding of our metaphor was suggested.[12] It seems that there is a children's circle game, where a circle is drawn, within which people are safe. Only when children venture outside the circle can someone "get" them. Perhaps we might think of our goal as that of turning our game into just such a "caring circle," where people are nurtured, refurbished so they can go bravely back outside the circle. If our goal is always to make the circle as big as possible and as welcoming as it can be to all who need it, we might be able to convince others to help build it, instead of always wanting to criticize it, tear it down, or shrink it. At least it may be worth a try.

The first step will be to take as strong a stance as possible in demanding public programs and a public responsibility for providing caring services. We will have to overcome our doubts about the state enough to recognize that a caring society depends upon using public resources to care for ourselves. Such a position does not mean no criticism. Rather it means criticism exactly because public programs are ours by rights and should always be better. It does not mean accepting big bureaucracies. If we have learned anything from the public/private relationships and the patterns of deinstitutionalization, it should be that public money can provide services in small settings as well as big ones. It does not mean

144 THE CIRCLE GAME

accepting hierarchical power structures without debate. Indeed, all the demand for public responsibility to care for human needs means is that we continually argue, urge, push, and organize to insist that the services people need should be provided by the taxes we all pay for our "general welfare."

Before we dismiss this as rhetorical flourish, we might spend time listening to talk shows. On most radio and TV shows in Boston during the fall of 1981, participants from the Coalition for Basic Human Needs—a welfare advocacy group—heard one consistent refrain. Over and over, people called in to say how miserable they were, and because they couldn't get help, no one else should either. Sample comments are important: "I work two jobs because I can't afford housing, medical bills, and my kids' education. Why should you get these for free?" or "I'm a single woman who has to spend an hour and a half getting back and forth to work and I have to leave my kids with a neighbor too much of the time. Why should I pay for you to stay home with your kids?" or "I'm retired and I had to work every day of my life at a job that I hated in order to take care of my family; and we never had much. Why should you think you can ask taxpayers like me to pay for your kids while you go to college to get a degree and have a better job than I ever had?"

Such experiences are powerful and sad. Our job is to acknowledge the pain and to offer another solution. Somehow we must find the words, and the programs, to turn some of that profound misery and jealousy back into social hope. We will not do this by further privatizing the response to such needs, as the Right suggests; instead, we must raise expectations so that people become more willing to pay (equitable) taxes to get some needs met and gain the sense that their concerns are valid enough so that they can demand more, not less, when they feel needy.

The second step will be to develop a set of long-range and short-range activities to "sell" the notion that public services are ours and that they should be good, because we deserve the best. Such arguments can be used to bolster tax-reform programs that are responsive to the reasons people voted for Proposition 2½, but that attempt to rearrange the overall tax structure so that adequate public money is available to fund needed services. A similar argument must be made at the federal level, along with criticism of the replacement of the welfare state with a warfare state.

Without giving up the fight for national programs, we may still use the "local approach" (forced upon us by the federal abdication of responsibility) to develop a keener sense of local public service priorities. Later a broader state and national strategy can perhaps be built that reflects local priorities. Here is where self help and alternative approaches may be tried, not out of a glorification of "independence," but as ways to develop models for demands for future funding. "Counter institutions" may also allow us to keep imagining how we would like things to be, a critical task in these mean-spirited times.[13]

Similarly, the crisis may be used within agencies to force re-thinking of how agency hierarchies divide workers from each other, limit agency flexibility, and stifle creativity. As adminis-trators and workers come under the same attack, now may be the time for service employees to push for more workplace control, in exchange for continued productivity and responsiveness to public needs.[14]

In specific agencies, some "visionary" strategies may be pushed, even if they may not be won. The goal should always be to create a sense of more options than those seemingly allowed by a dimin-ishing environment, not just to win in the short run. For exam-ple, within a Welfare Department without social services, there will be pressures during the 1980s to become more "managerial" than ever. Attempts will continue to be made to limit the per-sonal contacts between payments workers and clients, to decrease the number of places where people can apply for services, and to increase the number of forms clients must fill out. However, op-posite pressures may also be at work that could be supported by internal and external activists.

In the past, welfare offices often operated like "protection teams" in the old gangster movies, one good guy and one bad guy. The payments units would make people feel inadequate and un-trusted and then the service units would patch them up again. Without the service units, welfare workers and administrators could seek a new identity. Some are already looking for a "posi-tive image" for the new department, for a way to consider their activity "financial services." There may be a way to support this by pushing, whenever possible, the department to provide the "best service," to be more supportive of clients, and to spend en-ergy planning to distribute this service in the most accessible and friendly way. This would, of course, not fundamentally change the way welfare operates in this society, but it might change the image of the service, allow workers to do a more rewarding job, and help clients to feel less demoralized.

Similarly, attempts to instill forced-work requirements—work-fare—on AFDC recipients must be fought on many levels. Legal advocates may choose to focus just on stopping the plans, by whatever procedural means. Of course, such tactics are important to protect people. But even more sensible, in the long run, would be to use the workfare issue as a way to build old, but lost, alliances between workers and clients and to raise long-standing demands for governmental responsibility for full employment, not forced work. The hypocrisy of attempts to force women to work outside the home while denying services to other working women may be exposed. In short, even if we don't win immediately, struggles within and outside welfare in the 1980s can aim at changing expectations of the public sector.

Medicaid, too, may serve as an arena for widening definitions of social responsibility. Cuts aimed at eliminating recipient choice by forcing them into prepaid "charity wards" must be opposed, with arguments that insist upon the needs and the rights for a range of services. But new measures that emphasize that doctors, hospitals, nursing homes, and pharmacies have become part of the public sector, and can be held accountable, may be part of an effort to redefine public responsibility by first acknowledging which programs are already public.

The new Department of Social Services must be constantly pressured to drop its "child-saving" focus and to stress the other side of its initial appeal, the role of providing needed and desired services to a wide range of people. The agency may still be able to provide an important role—especially as block grants allow more autonomy, if less money—in combining the advocacy role, previously belonging to the Office for Children, with the role of providing as many services as possible. The agency, for example, might take a leadership stance in pushing public schools to take over day care provision—a forgotten demand of the *Children's Puzzle* that could lead to greater public identity with social services.

Deinstitutionalization would be reviewed without either retreating to an institutional approach—as some unionists have done—or blindly defending the current system. If the goal is to develop a widespread sense of the importance of public services, then the goal of excellent community care is a critical piece of the plan to rebuild public trust. If the general public sees good facilities in the community they may begin to identify with them—much as cities and towns previously felt connected to "their" welfare office. The trick is to offer a range of programs so that people may be appropriately served and to push the notion that people have rights to the most effective treatment.

Contracted services, also, may become a part of a general strategy to revive public sector responsibility .They do not have to be opposed in principal. Rather, they need to be included as part of an expanded notion of a public system, not as something private outside of it. In other words, when it seems best to use purchased services they should be offered (to provide greater flexibility of approaches, for instance). But they remain one part of the public's responsibility for caring, not something that the "private" sector does for the inept government. And, of course, contracting can be opposed when it only serves as a means to "dump" clients and avoid public obligations. Certainly unions need to continue to seek ways to organize employees in contracted agencies, in order to avoid two tiers of workers with the resulting divisiveness.

The movement of DYS toward a narrow "juvenile corrections" approach, instead of toward its earlier mission as a "services" agency, must be opposed. Workers, administrators, and advocates need to wage a campaign to oppose this retreat from ten years of reform and broadening of public responsibility.

The Office for Children has seemingly been abandoned since 1978. Perhaps its advocacy functions can best be fulfilled by DSS, especially with real pressures imposed by budget cutbacks. What seems important is that children's advocates find ways to keep the earlier vision alive, a vision that insisted that children had rights to a wide range of decent services and that all agencies of the state system must be held accountable in regard to fulfilling those rights.

Similarly, the Department of Elder Affairs may be forced to revive its initial promise of advocacy for elders. Under the pressure of "economic realities" elderly groups and area agencies may find themselves fighting each other, when they need to be collectively watching proposals to change Medicaid, for instance. Here the elderly have an advantage: they seem already to have a widespread public base. The ideal would be for elderly advocates to use their leadership position within the "circle of caring" to reach out and bring in others. If elderly leaders could insist that they are "poor people" too, that their concerns for public responsiveness include concerns for women and children on welfare, that they want to share with children the use of public school facilities, then an important discussion could take place in the public arena.

Reorganization plans may again cause confusion for those wanting increased public responsibility in the 1980s. Already one major plan has been developed, although it seems to be stalled.[15] We cannot anticipate all proposals, but a few observations can be made. Proposals that Medicaid be moved to the Department of Public Health should be supported, because of the experience of Public Health as an entitlement agency, serving everyone. Like the shift of elderly and disabled categories to SSI, the shift of Medicaid to Public Health could be a step toward enhancing the public desirability of health supports. It might also end the confusion about how expensive welfare is. Conversely, efforts to split EOHS may not be so positive because they might further a division between "worthy and unworthy" services. However, the important thing is that activists should not take a merely reactive stance toward reorganizations. The lessons from our study show that such efforts can sometimes mean real improvements in the rationality of the system and in the ways in which human services are presented to the general public. Because our goal is to create a system that is attractive and makes sense to the people to whom it belongs, reorganization efforts can be worthwhile.

Fighting for economic survival will surely be a priority for trade unionists during the 1980s. But activists need to look for ways to help human service unions take more leadership in the substantive areas of service delivery, in defining the role of contracted agencies, and in fights for client dignity. Grand and informal as such suggestions sound, they will be critical directions if public service workers are to reassert their credibility to themselves and to the general public. The unions should take positions on substantive proposals and testify about them before the legislature and before the public. The purpose is not mere window dressing, but is, instead, part of a massive effort to assert that the people who do the work of human services have informed and serious opinions about the quality of services and about their public obligation to provide good services.

Welfare client organizing has stepped up since 1978, with the statewide Coalition for Basic Human Needs (CBHN) taking a leadership role. It is easy to call for support and unity with groups like CBHN, but not clear how workers or nonrecipient activists can achieve it. Here we only suggest that welfare recipients might do well to ally with elderly groups, if possible, in order to force a public recognition of all the people (old people, children, and women) who use services. While alliances with the elderly won't be easy, neither will worker alliances. Perhaps for the present, workers and clients should organize separately. All-client groups may be best able to make a public appeal to expose the immoral implications of "moral-majority" cuts and to insist on their rights to basic care.

One of the troubles with political tactics is that, especially in times of crisis, nothing seems like enough and everything should have been done yesterday. The frustration with any list, such as the one just provided, is that, clearly, no one tactic alone will work. Even worse, it is not obvious how to link them into a unified strategy of expanding public responsibility. One likely prospect may keep us going, however, and may give us the energy to devise new tactics as needed. It is the specter of the next game (maybe we should call it the End Game) that will be played if we lose. If we cannot re-establish the premise of public responsibility for service delivery and if the New Right wins its ideological battles, human services will then become *only* the social-control instruments they now have the potential to be. And human service workers will be nothing but the prison guards of the new system. Whatever slim hopes existed for the Circle Game to be caring and constantly changing will be gone. We simply cannot allow this to happen.

We interviewed a black woman who had been a nurse and a neighborhood service worker for twenty years. She was also a foster parent and community activist. When we asked her how she kept going she replied:

I don't know what else to do. The programs are still bad, people are still hurting, and the rules are still unfair. But I won't give them the satisfaction of thinking they have won. In my [mental health] clinic, they have to deal with me. I've been there too long and I've got too many contacts in the community. Sometimes we've even been able to stop the worst plans for our area. And when we didn't win, we didn't lose as bad as we would have if nobody opposed them.

Who knows. Maybe someday people will be more together again. Then I'll be there. It's just something you have to keep doing once you start.

Appendix

A   Method of Inquiry

This study began in January 1979, as Governor Michael Dukakis's administration ended and Edward King's began. At that time the work was planned as a "pamphlet" that would document the history of events since the mid-sixties, when the contemporary system of services emerged, until the King administration, when—as I said at the time—"a new stage was beginning" for Massachusetts human services. Although I did not foresee the future Reagan administration's policies, nor the passage of Proposition 2½, I was not alone in recognizing that the philosophy and style of the new governor would herald a significant break with the recent past for human services in Massachusetts.

Why a history? Why not a standard policy analysis or a more statistically "rigorous" study of program implementation?

For me, the answer was a clear "Why not?" I had been peripherally involved in the Massachusetts human services arena since 1970 and had been constantly aware of my own need to know a chronology of the development of programs with which I worked. As a teacher, administrator, trainer, researcher, and consultant I had found my own spotty knowledge to be mirrored by that of workers and administrators. We all came and went within different parts of the system, but were woefully unaware of the patterns we were repeating, the lessons that might have been learned from the past.

Indeed, I had gone to a graduate school of social welfare in part out of a need for such history. There I found a history of national endeavors but little documentation of state efforts. I learned to do policy analyses of state programs, but often found them too dry, aimed at high-level decision makers, not the employees, clients, and concerned citizens who do the day-to-day work of human services. So I had long wanted to pull together a local history, and, as Massachusetts faced an inevitable new series of changes, the time seemed right to create a "base-line" work, to provide an accessible narrative of where we were and how we got there before the new era began.

I recruited a group of thirteen students, all themselves current or past workers in the system, and we set out on a joint research project "to get the story straight." Our initial goal was one of fact gathering. I operated as team leader, and the group read back issues of the *Boston Globe,* collected dusty reports from various agencies, and reviewed the few published studies of the agencies under review. No private documents were used. Everything collected was either published for public consumption or was widely circulated as internal agency reports or memos. Always the goal was to organize known data, not to look for any exposé of hidden motives or machinations. Much of our time was initially spent in weekly meetings where we tried to understand the chronology and to compare parallel developments across agencies.

By mid-semester, we gleefully covered the blackboard with a time line and began to feel that we understood the basic chain of events. From then on our task became both more interesting and more complex. We wanted to make sense of our story, to explain the dynamics and repercussions of change from the differing perspectives of participants. Research team members learned "oral-history" techniques from a resident historian and then interviewed each other, both to see how to ask questions and to add the groups' memories to the record.

After we felt ready, many of the students and I began to interview. We put a notice in the college's "Info Sheet" and contacted other friends outside the university. As the semester went on we sought out people who worked in areas that we had not yet covered. Finally, by mid-summer thirty people had been interviewed, including members of the team. Group interviews occurred at the college. Individual interviews were held both at school and away. Some of the interviews, particularly the group discussions, were taped. Team members learned how to keep notes during interviews and how to write detailed notes after interviews. This method proved most useful, especially because we made an early decision not to use names, so exact quotation was less crucial.

In all, I participated in interviews with twenty people in this group. Ten interviews were conducted without me. Of the thirty people interviewed, seventeen were workers and lower-level administrators in public and some private agencies. Eight were current or past recipients of some public service. Five were activists who worked as organizers around human-service issues.

We also interviewed thirty people who were at the higher end of the spectrum of human service activity. Some were obvious choices—all relevant commissioners were interviewed, for instance. Others were selected because their names were mentioned by several people, or because I or a member of the research team knew of their role. With half it seemed appropriate to name them as interviewees because their perspectives were influential to the period and the study. For others it served no purpose to mention names, either because of concern for confidentiality or simply because people's remarks were not central in influencing our understanding of the issues.

Most of the interviews with upper and middle-level administrators were held in the spring and summer of 1979. I conducted all these interviews, although often another research team member was present. I did not use a tape recorder at these interviews, for fear of inhibiting discussion. Again, notes were taken during the interviews and extensive process notes written directly afterward. My own prior service work, my research background at Brandeis, and my academic preparation in history all had given me a "trained ear" so that the interview records are reflective of what was said. Because the interview data was to be used to enliven the record, not for the presentation of factual information, such a method was more than adequate.

During the fall of 1979, I organized all the material, conducted a few final interviews, and wrote a first draft of what had become, not a pamphlet, but an eighty-page "booklet." I distributed this to the research team, to colleagues, some interviewees and to a group of thirty students who were taking a course on "Human Services in Massachusetts," which I taught in the spring of 1980. This first draft was overloaded with facts and difficult to follow. However, most of my readers were energetic editors, full of suggestions for how to make the story more relevant, more accessible. (I think many of the students, especially, enjoyed helping their teacher correct such a clearly unacceptable manuscript.)

As a result of comments on the first draft, I interviewed five more recipients and decided to expand the document into a more general treatment suitable for a book. A second draft was ready by January 1981 and suffered a scrutiny similar to that given the first draft. In the fall of 1981 a final revision was prepared and completed in January 1982.

Thus, what was to have been a short pamphlet became a book of over 100 pages. The goal of providing an accessible and useful history remained the same, although the form changed and the scope broadened due to a growing awareness of the background needed to "make sense" of the story. In addition, as national and state policies changed drastically, it became necessary to reassess my judgments and to look for heretofore hidden roots of the present within the original story. The intellectual and political issues this posed were mentioned in chapter

1. Here they are described again to help explain why it took such a long time to prepare a document that began with the simple purpose of setting the record straight!

Interviewees

1. The following individuals were interviewed and their insights proved important enough to the conception of the manuscript that their names are included here. None are ever quoted by name in the document and all represented themselves, not their agencies, in the interview: Martin Abramowitz (Welfare), Lois Balfour (union-welfare), Douglas Baird (private provider), James Callahan (Medicaid/aging), Robert Curtis (Mental Health/Area Strategy), Hubie Jones (private provider/educator), Al Kramer (state-level generalist), Lillie Landrum (welfare advocacy), Steven Minter (Welfare), Robert Okin (Mental Health), Robert Ott (Welfare/federal perspective), Francis Sargent (governor), Mel Scovell (Medicaid), Al Sharp (Welfare), Jerald Stevens (Welfare/EOHS), Chela Tawa (professional advocate).

2. Fifteen individuals were interviewed who held positions of some responsibility within the management of public and private agencies. They remain anonymous to avoid recognition or because their ideas are not strongly reflected in the document. The categorical breakdown of this group is:

Category	Number interviewed
Welfare/Medicaid/Social Services	5
Mental Health	3
Office for Children	2
Department of Youth Services	1
Nonstate agencies	4

3. Seventeen people were interviewed who were students of the College of Public and Community Services or friends of students who work as direct-service workers in a range of agencies. The categorical breakdown of this group is:

Category	Number interviewed
Welfare workers	5
Mental Health	3
Office for Children	2
Division of Youth Services	2
Day care (private contracted program)	2
Homemaker service	1
Elderly services	1
Alcoholism services	2

4. Twelve people were interviewed who were recipients of services. The categorical breakdown for this group is:

Category	Number interviewed
Welfare recipients	7
Children's services	2
Mental health services	2
Rehabilitation services	1

5. Five people interviewed were activists and organizers for community and social services.

B Massachusetts Human Service Expenditures and Populations, FY 1981 Massachusetts Population—5,728,000

Agency	Appropriation[1]	Population served [2]	
		Total population served (includes	
Executive Office of Human Services	2,636,579,545	duplication)	1.7m[4]
Department of Public Welfare	1,744 m	Total DPW	590,000
Aid to Families with Dependent Children	533 m	123,000 families	333,000
General Relief	51 m		22,000
Transfer to SSI	125 m		123,000
Medicaid [5]	940 m		590,000
Other (administrative costs, food stamp administration, emergency assistance, emergency needs)	95 m		
Department of Mental Health	438 m	(65,652 at one time)	281,000
State hospitals for the mentally ill	67.2m		2,115
Community services for the mentally ill	114.3m		258,000
State schools for the retarded	94.5m		4,225
Community services for the retarded	61.2m		18,000
Other			
Department of Social Services	180 m[6]		265,000
Title XX	130.5		
Child welfare	49.5		
Department of Public Health	105 m		350,000
Department of Youth Services	26.2m	ca. 1,900 caseload 56% between 16-17	3,000
Office for Children	5.9m		50,000
Massachusetts Rehabilitation	5.6m[7]		35,000
All other EOHS Programs	131.2m		
Department of Corrections	62.1		
Commission for the Blind	30.4		
Veterans Services	25.5		
Rate Setting	1.5		
Executive Office of Elder Affairs Only State	57,030,019		36,000
Department of Elder Affairs State & Federal	68 m[8]		30,000
Home Care Corporations	68 m		
Federal money channeled through services for elderly (OAA-Title XX)	16.9m		
Administration	.5m		

Number of state employees[3]	Notes

1 In order to achieve some level of comparability with Appendix C, the appropriation figures used here are taken from the Massachusetts Taxpayers Foundation, *State Budget Trends 1973–1982* (Boston, 1981). It must be noted that there are disparities between these figures and those provided in the "Plan to Reorganize Massachusetts Human Services for the 1980's" from the Executive Office of Human Services, July 1981. Most differences were minor (taken as a portion of the whole) and seemed to result from differences between allocations and actual expenditures.

4,500

2 The numbers of people served are taken from the "Plan to Reorganize." For DMH, there was a great discrepancy with figures printed in the Blue Ribbon Commission, *Mental Health Crossroads*, S. Stephen Rosenfeld, chairperson (May 1981). The DMH figure of 281,000 was used instead of the EOHS figure of 400,000.

19,000

3 The figures for numbers of state employees are taken from the "Plan to Reorganize" except for DPW, where they were omitted. A call to DPW's personnel office yielded the figure of 4,500 listed here.

4 When I try to take duplication into account, I arrive at an estimate of approximately 750,000 people using services. See chap. 2, n. 2.

5 AFDC and Medicaid costs are reimbursed at about a 50 percent rate by the federal government.

6 Breakdown for DSS comes from their budget office because of conflicts over sources of funds. The total Title XX budget in 1981 was $190 million, more than the entire DSS budget.

2,427

The $50 million in Title XX services delivered by Home Care Corporations do not appear in the DSS budget, nor do the moneys contracted to other state agencies. The only Title XX money that is part of the DSS budget is that which

4,345

532

it directly administers or contracts for. (Conversation with Consuela Faust, DSS)

7 The figures for the Massachusetts Rehabilitation Commission's federal funds came from the agency, because the Massachusetts Taxpayers Foundation and EOHS were so at odds. (Neither, finally, was in agreement with MRC figures.)

90

8 The breakdown for DEA comes from the department budget office, because all published sources were quite confused in their presentation of the different sources of DEA funds (Bob Gill, DEA).

C   Expenditures and Population, Selected Massachusetts Human Service Programs 1966–1978*

Agency	1966 Population	1966 % Human service budget and expenditure	1970 Population
Executive Office of Human Services	No EOHS	385.4m[1] (280.2)	
Department of Public Welfare		61% (46%) 233.7m[5] (128.5)	
AFDC	132,000	60.9m	228,000
GR	8,580	9.2m	19,700
SSI (Old Age/Disability)	63,000	82.8m	76,030
Medicaid	30,000	69.4m	229,500
Social Services	8,260	7.3m	12,100
Other		4.1m	
Department of Mental Health		22% (31%) 84.9m[7]	
Hospitals for Mentally Ill	19,100	56.7m	16,950
Schools for the Retarded	17,682	18.1m	7,095
Community Programs		1.9m	
Other		8.2m	
Department of Public Health		8% (11%) 31.3m	
Department of Youth Services		1% (2%)	
	1,000	4.2m[9]	
Office for Children	No OFC		No OFC
Massachusetts Rehabilitation[10] Commission		2.3m	
Other EOHS Programs		8% (10%) 2.9m	
Commission for the Blind		4.1m	
Corrections		12.9m	
Veteran Services		12.0m	
Executive Office of Elder Affairs	No DEA		No DEA
Department of Elder Affairs	(Commission on Aging—research funds—$30,000)		(Welfare social services for the elderly—$400,000)

* See Appendix D for inflation controlled growth figures

	1974		1978	
% Human service budget and expenditure	Population	% Human service budget and expenditure	Population	% Human service budget and expenditure
904.1m[2]		1370.7m[3]		1950.0m[4]
70%		74%		76%
630.5m[6]		1014.6m		1478.1m
172.2m	336,000	305.6m	367,000	489.3m
36.1m	29,000	60.0m	20,000	45.2m
103.1m	87,700	99.0m	129,600	117.2m
252.2m	357,000	382.0m	597,000	644.9m
19.9m		39.5m		91.5m
43.3m		65.0m		90.0m
14%		14%		14%
122.4m[8]		188.4m		272.9m
83.5m	7,000	93.4m	2,900	89.7m
29.3m	5,000	49.4m	5,000	69.0m
13.3m		36.2m		99.8m
		8.4m		14.6m
5%		5%		4%
41.0m		68.7m		77.1m
1%		1%		1%
6.0m		17.9m		18.0m
		4.3m		4.8m
2.5m	30,000	3.2m	39,000	4.7m
11%		5%		5%
99.1m		73.6m		94.5m
6.0m		9.7m		16.7m
18.7m		32.4m		47.5m
15.6m		19.2m		18.4m
		3.0m		27.7m[11]
		3.0m	32,000	

Notes

1   Figures for 1966 are sometimes confusing. The larger figure is a total for all human service costs for the programs listed, as taken from Massachusetts Taxpayers Foundation, *State Budget Trends 1965–1973* (Boston, 1973), and

from the Commonwealth of Massachusetts, *Financial Report, 1966*, published by the comptroller's office. The second figure (in parentheses) does not count the federal money that went to public assistance programs, because, at the time, this money went directly to cities and towns and never appeared in the state budget.

2   This number is taken from the Massachusetts Taxpayers Foundation, *State Budget Trends 1965–1973*. It is smaller than the 918 million given later in *State Budget Trends 1966–1975*, but larger than the numbers seem to indicate in the 1970 *Financial Report*. The differences are probably attributable to varied ways of counting federal expenditures.

3   This figure is taken from figures in *FY 75 Budget: Summary of Programs and Recommendations* or *The Budget in English*, published by the Sargent administration. The budget analysis in this exemplary document was used for all the 1974 statistics here, so this total was used, even though it differs by 28 million from the 1,398.6 million used in the *State Budget Trends*. Here the discrepancies are probably due to the use of allocations instead of exact expenditures in the *FY 75 Budget*.

4   Massachusetts Taxpayers Foundation, *State Budget Trends 1971–1980* (Boston, 1980) was used for all figures for this year.

5   These numbers are taken from the Department of Public Welfare *Annual Statistical Report FY 1968*, except for the Social Service and Administrative Costs, which come from the *State Budget Trends 1965–1973*. It is also important to remember that 45 percent of all welfare costs were supported by the federal government, 33 percent by the state, and 21 percent by local governments in 1966.

6   These expenditures and population figures are taken from the Department of Public Welfare *Annual Report (1971)*, except for the Social Service and administrative costs, which come from the *State Budget Trends 1965–1973*.

7   This total figure and the total institutional population count comes from *State Budget Trends 1965–1973*.

8   *State Budget Trends 1965–1973*.

9   In 1966, youth services were provided under the Department of Education, so this figure appeared in their budget. See *State Budget Trends 1965–1973*.

10   Mass. Rehab. budget figures are deceptive for all years because of the large amount of federal grant money administered by the department and not appearing in the state budget. In 1966 and 1970 federal grant money exceeded $8 million; in 1974 it was greater than $12 million; and in 1978 greater than $20 million.

11   The large increase in DEA funds is attributable, in part, to a new method of counting social service costs to the elderly, as part of the DEA budget, instead of the DPW budget.

D   Human Service Spending as Percent of State Spending
and State Spending in Current and Constant Dollars, 1966–1980 [1]

1966		1970	
Total State Budget	771m	Total State Budget	1.8b
Human Services (does not include federal welfare reimbursements or costs of local welfare contributions)	34%	Human Services	49%
Welfare (state costs)	10%[2]	Welfare	35%[2]
Mental Health	11%	Mental Health	7%
Public Health	4%	Public Health	2%
Other	9%	Other	5%
Education (including Youth Services)	18%	Education	24%
Treasury (debts, pensions)	17%	Treasury (debts, pensions)	8%
Transportation	7%	A&F	5%
Other	24%	Other	14%

1975		1980	
Total State Budget	3.6b	Total State Budget	5.5b
Human Services	45%	Human Services	42%
Welfare (excluding federal share of SSI)	36%[2]	Welfare (excluding federal share of SSI)	31%[2]
Mental Health	6%	Mental Health	7%
Public Health	2%	Public Health	2%
Other	1%	Other	2%
Education	27%	Education	22%
Treasury (debts, pensions)	8%	Treasury (debts, pensions)	11%
A&F	7%	A&F	12%
Other	13%	Other	13%

[1] Source: Jeff Singleton, "Impact of Fiscal Crisis on State Spending, Services and Taxes," unpublished report for Policy Training Center (Boston, 1980).
[2] Of total state budget.

State Spending in Current and Constant Dollars (1961–1980)

Billions

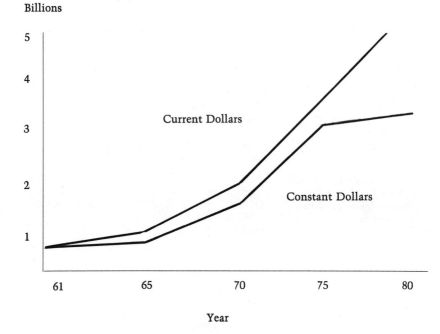

Year

Source: Jeff Singleton, "Impact of Fiscal Crisis on State Spending, Services and Taxes," taken from Massachusetts Taxpayers Foundation, *Budget Trends 1966–'75* and *Budget Trends 1971–'80.*

E   Meeting the Problems of People in Massachusetts

In 1965 the National Study Service made a total of fifty-four recommendations in *Meeting the Problems of People in Massachusetts: A Study of the Massachusetts Public Welfare System*. In addition, a whole new structure was proposed for delivering social services. Here I have chosen those major recommendations that seem most central to the study.

Recommendations:

The Commonwealth should assume responsibility for the portion of cost now being provided locally (and along with it the administrative responsibility which should follow state financing) (p. 59).

The First Major Goal. The first task will obviously be to lay out plans for bringing together present programs at a common administrative level. It would appear that the first major goal in the transition should be the successful coordination and where feasible, integration, of present programs under the new administrative structure. As the department resolves questions of structure and program relationships, and as it makes the many administrative decisions and procedural plans relating to the administrative services necessary to maintain these programs, it will be setting down patterns and laying out relationships which will lend themselves to the absorption of broader programs, and new services as they are added (p. 84).

The law requiring a mother to take court action against a father for the purpose of obtaining support payments, in order to attain continuing eligibility for assistance, should be eliminated (p. 18).

The basic standards of need used for budgeting purposes in public assistance should be carefully reviewed and revised in accordance with present-day patterns of consumption and changing concepts of adequacy. Steps should be taken to assure more consistent use of the special needs items, and those items in the standard budget which are not meeting needs should be revised upwards (p. 18).

The effort that Massachusetts had made to lower case loads of workers so that they can have more time to provide effective service to clients should be continued (p. 24).

The current efforts to train public assistance staff must be redoubled all up and down the line (p. 24).

Special efforts must be made to improve services in Aid to Families with Dependent Children where needs are serious and present services appear to be less effective than in other categories (p. 24).

The State Department of Public Welfare should be given a clear legal mandate to develop and administer a program of social services to assist families and protect children throughout the Commonwealth who are confronted with the social, physical, and emotional problems requiring such protection (p. 35).

The State Department of Public Welfare should be given a clearly mandated responsibility to assess unmet needs in services for children and families, to make needs known, and to provide leadership, community by community, in stimulating new approaches and in development of needed services, both under its own auspices and under the auspices of voluntary agencies (p. 35).

The name, "Division of Child Guardianship" should be changed to one more descriptive of its broad charge. "Division of Services for Children and Youth," "Division of Child Care and Protection," or "Division of Social Services for Families and Children" are suggestions (p. 35).

Licensing of group day care facilities should be transferred from the State Department of Health to the State Department of Public Welfare. Day care is an important part of a total child-welfare program. Primary leadership and program development responsibility would be more effective if concentrated in a single regulatory agency (p. 36).

Physical facilities and working conditions have a direct bearing on effective use of present scarce staff, and on recruitment and retention of staff of the caliber needed to man this complex and important professional service. Attention to these facilitating factors is urgently required (p. 36).

The personnel responsibilities for public welfare in respect to classification, selection, salary allocation, and appeals, should be centralized (p. 54).

Minimum educational requirements should be established and continuous recruitment should be maintained (p. 54).

Vigorous steps should be taken to change the poor image of employment in the public social services in Massachusetts. This can only be done by making the program goals, the job opportunities, and the working conditions more compatible with attainment of sound professional goals and expectations (p. 54). A unified training plan should be prepared and implemented. It should include provision for orientation of all new workers and new supervisors, as well as of old workers or supervisors who need orientation to new concepts or new jobs (p. 57).

F   Recommendations of *The Children's Puzzle*

The Children's Services Task Force, Institute for Governmental Services, University of Massachusetts/Boston, was headed by David Sheehan. It produced *The Children's Puzzle: A Study of Services to Children in Massachusetts* in 1977 and made twenty-three recommendations to Representative John J. Finnegan, Chairman of the House Ways and Means Committee. The ten recommendations most relevant to our analysis were:

The Department of Public Welfare should be abolished. All social service programs should be transferred to a new department to be named the Department of Human Development. All assistance payment programs should be transferred to a new department to be named the Department of Economic Security. The new department should include two divisions: the Division of Employment Security and the Division of Family and Individual Assistance.

The Department of Youth Services should be abolished. All DYS programs should be transferred to the new Department of Human Development.

The Department of Mental Health should be divided among two agencies: all programs related to mental retardation should be transferred to a new department to be named the Department of Rehabilitative Services; all other Department of Mental Health programs should become the foundation of the new Department of Human Development.

The Department of Public Health programs related to crippled children (except pre-schools for crippled children) and the responsibility for pediatric nursing-home programs should be transferred to the new Department of Rehabilitative Services.

The Massachusetts Rehabilitation Commission, the Commission for the Blind and the Bureau of Developmental Disabilities should be transferred to the new Department of Rehabilitative Services.

The Office for Children should be abolished as a state agency. The licensing function and the flexible children's monies should be transferred to the new Department of Human Development.

A quasi-public corporation should replace the Office for Children. The new organization should be governed by a Board of Directors consisting of fifteen members all of whom should be appointed by the Governor. The new organization should make annual reports to the Governor and the Legislature on the status of services to children; it should be empowered by stature to be an advocate for children, to represent children before any state agency and to initiate legal action against any state agency which is determined not to be in compliance with the laws of the Commonwealth.

The Department of Human Development, the Department of Rehabilitative Services, and the Department of Public Health should all have congruent regional and area boundaries. The state should be divided into six regions and forty areas.

Each of the forty human service areas should have an area board of consumers, professionals and child providers for each of the three Departments of Human

Development, Rehabilitative Service and Public Health. The area boards should establish priorities within the guidelines of state policy and should have a designated area budget.

The Secretary of Human Services should be empowered to establish uniform contracting procedures and uniform intake and referral forms; to establish uniform standards for monitoring and evaluating all human service programs; and to establish standard licensing procedures for the Departments of Human Development, Rehabilitative Services, and Public Health.

G   Glossary and Common Acronyms

Aid to Families with Dependent Children (AFDC)—a federal program funded under Title IV of the Social Security Act (originally named Aid to Dependent Children—ADC). The federal government under the Department of Health and Human Services (HHS)—previously Health, Education and Welfare (HEW)—provides eligibility standards and reimburses the state for approximately 50 percent of its costs in income supports to children and eligible adults who care for them. No adult is eligible without having an eligible child in his or her home. The program is administered by the Department of Public Welfare (DPW) with federal guidelines but with limited options to alter benefits. (Source: *Income Maximization Manual for the Poor, the Aging, and Those Getting Poorer in Massachusetts*, 3d ed., Community Advocates Law Office, Boston, 1980)

A&F—Executive Office of Administration and Finance

The Alliance—the organization representing Massachusett's two major public sector unions, the Service Employees International Union (SEIU) and the American Federation of State, County and Municipal Employees (AFSCME). Formed in 1975, the Alliance engages in collective bargaining with the state and represents most public sector employees directly hired by the state—except higher education faculty and nurses.

Area Strategy—a statewide reform effort during 1977–78, which was instituted with the support of the Executive Office of Human Services, aimed at decentralizing services delivery and service planning.

Chapter 766—an act, passed in 1972, which requires that all Massachuseets school systems provide special education services. The Department of Education provides support funding according to a reimbursement formula. This act offered another avenue for advocates seeking more services for children.

Children in Need of Services (CHINS)—a program authorized in 1973 to provide services for children between the ages of six and sixteen who are runaways, truants, or beyond parental control, but not legally delinquent. CHINS decriminalized "status offenders" and redefined their problems as service needs. The program was administered by DPW until 1980, when it came under the jurisdiction of the Department of Social Services (DSS). (Source: *Income Maximization Manual* and author's description)

The Comprehensive Employment and Training Act (CETA)—a federal act, passed in 1973, that provides job training and employment opportunities for low-income unemployed or underemployed people. It consolidated many previously existing programs under one umbrella. Major cities are "prime sponsors" and receive money directly from the federal government. Smaller cities and towns receive money that is channeled through the Executive Office of Manpower Affairs. (Source: *Income Maximization Manual* and author's description)

Contracted services—a term used to describe those services that state agencies do not provide directly themselves, but that they fund through contracts to nonprofit or appropriate private agencies.

DEA—Department of Elderly Affairs

Deinstitutionalization—the general policy developed whereby youth services, mental health, and retardation services are moved from large state institutions into a system of "community services." Such services may be provided while individuals reside in private living arrangements or in small facilities—such as halfway houses, community residences, or runaway homes.

DES—Department of Employment Security

Division of Child Guardianship (DCG)—a program within DPW, from 1953 through 1971, that received and planned for the use of federal funds for child welfare. DCG provided direct services to children and families, paid fees for services to selected private agencies and licensed private child placement agencies, child-caring institutions, and families providing foster care. In 1971 it became the Social Services Unit within DPW. (Source: *Meeting the Problems of People in Massachusetts*, National Study Service, 1965, and author's description)

DMH—Department of Mental Health

Donated funds—a mechanism whereby private agencies provide all or part of the money needed to match federal dollars available for service delivery. It allows state agencies to purchase service without expenditure of state funds.

DPH—Department of Public Health

DPW—Department of Public Welfare

DSS—Department of Social Services

DYS—Department of Youth Services

Emergency Assistance (EA)—a federal program that provides matching funds for aid necessary to meet certain "immediate and urgent" needs. The definition of such needs and the amount of aid available has changed often during the period under review. (Source: *Income Maximization Manual*)

EOHS—Executive Office of Human Services

Error rate—a formula whereby a rate of departmental error in determining eligibility and benefit levels is calculated. The "error rate" includes an accounting of many types of errors, not just those that result in overpayment, and was a source of tension between federal and state authorities during much of the period under review.

Flat grant—the quarterly allotment, initiated in 1970, to provide for general coverage for "special needs" of all recipients. Before it was implemented individual recipients could apply for a variety of special allotments. In 1980, the quarterly grant was discontinued and the amount provided was given as part of the monthly grant.

Food stamps—a federal program funded through the Department of Agriculture to supplement the food allotment for low-income individuals. The program has been administered statewide by DPW since 1974. Food vouchers—or stamps—are issued to eligible individuals and can be redeemed for allowable food products at participating stores. (Source: *Income Maximization Manual*)

General Relief (GR)—a totally state-funded program administered by DPW to provide minimal income to individuals and families who are unemployed and not eligible for other forms of public assistance. GR was almost totally funded by cities and towns until 1968. (Source: *Income Maximization Manual*)

General Relief–Medical Assistance (GR–MA)—a totally state-funded program, administered by DPW, which provides payment of medical bills for medical services and items. It is more structured in allowable benefits than Medicaid. (Source: *Income Maximization Manual*)

MCB—Massachusetts Commission for the Blind

MRC—Massachusetts Rehabilitation Commission (Mass. Rehab)

Medicaid (MA)—a federal needs-based entitlement program passed in 1965— Title XIX of the Social Security Act—which allows certain poor people to receive medical services. States have the discretion to limit the amount, scope, and duration of Medicaid-funded services. Administered by DPW, Medicaid pays full costs of allowable Medicaid expenses. (Source: *Income Maximization Manual*)

Mothers for Adequate Welfare (MAWs)—the local welfare advocacy group founded in Boston in 1965.

National Welfare Rights Organization (NWRO)—the national organization of welfare recipients, founded by George Wiley in 1966. A Massachusetts chapter (MWRO) was established in 1967 and developed a strategy, known as the "Boston Plan," for demanding more services for existing welfare recipients. (Source: Lawrence Bailis, *Bread or Justice: Grassroots Organizing in the Welfare Rights Movement*, Lexington, Mass.: D.C. Heath, 1974)

OASDI—Old Age, Survivors and Disability Insurance (Social Security)

OFC—Office for Children

Older Americans Act (OAA)—a federal act, passed in 1965, that provides funding for local coordination for the elderly as well as for nutrition and other limited services. Money is routed through DEA, but does not show in its budget. (Source: *Encyclopedia of Social Work*, ed. Turner et al. Washington, D.C.: National Association of Social Workers, 1976)

Provider agency—the term for an agency that receives state contracts or fees for services from state agencies in order to provide services to eligible clients. In 1976, many of the nonprofit provider agencies joined together to form the Massachusetts Council of Human Service Providers (MCHSP), an umbrella group that attempts to negotiate contract provisions and reforms with the state, on behalf of member agencies. (Source: Massachusetts Taxpayers Foundation, *Purchase of Service: Can State Government Gain Control?*, Boston, 1980)

Separation—the term used to describe the separation of social service workers and functions from financial payments workers and functions within the Department of Public Welfare. Although requested by federal authorities since 1967, separation of functions did not occur until 1974 in Massachusetts.

Social Security Act—the basic federal act, passed in 1935, that provides AFDC (Title IV), Medicaid (Title XIX), Social Services (Title XX), and child-welfare services. The act also authorizes the Social Security Old Age, Survivors' Disability Insurance (OASDI), unemployment insurance, and Medicare. (Source: *Encyclopedia of Social Work*)

Supplemental Security Income (SSI)—the federal program, begun in 1974, that provides "minimum income" for individuals, couples, and children who meet financial standards and are old, blind, or disabled. It replaced earlier public assistance programs that had been administered by DPW, with federal reimbursement. SSI is administered by the Social Security Administration (SSA). Though the eligibility criteria are the same throughout all fifty states, Massachusetts has elected to supplement the federally funded benefits through state legislation. (Source: *Income Maximization Manual*)

State takeover—the term used to describe the July 1968 state assumption of local welfare programs. It meant that all city and town welfare workers became state employees and that the state took over all nonfederal costs relating to GR, AFDC, and Medicaid.

Title IV—the provision of the Social Security Act that funds AFDC.

Title XIX—the provision of the Social Security Act that funds Medicaid.

Title XX—the provision of the Social Security Act that funds social services, now under the jurisdiction of the Department of Social Services, previously administered by DPW.

Special Supplemental Food Supplement Program for Women and Children (WIC) —a federal program created in 1972 to provide specific nutritional food supplements to women and children who are determined to be at "nutritional risk." The program is administered by a combination of federal, state, and local agencies. Federally, it is overseen by the Department of Agriculture. In Massachusetts it is managed by the Department of Public Health which identifies local vendors to become responsible for taking applicants and distributing food supplements. (Source: *Income Maximization Manual*)

Work Incentive Program (WIN)—a work and training program first enacted in 1967, for the purpose of assisting AFDC recipients in obtaining and maintaining self-sufficiency through adequate employment. It was jointly administered by DPW, which provided support services, and the Division of Employment Security, which provided manpower services. In 1982 it was replaced with a modified program. (Source: *Income Maximization Manual*)

Workfare—a general term used to describe programs that require welfare recipients to do public service work in exchange for their welfare checks. First proposed in Massachusetts in 1975, it resulted at that time in a small program limited to GR recipients and unemployed fathers on AFDC. An expanded program is proposed for 1982.

Notes

1 Introduction

1 I am indebted to Scott Bass of the College of Public and Community Service for his complex understanding of the social psychology of what he calls the "fraternity" of upper-level administrators.

2 See *Is There Life after 2½?* (1981), a publication of the Policy Training Center, 10 West Street, Boston, Mass.; and Martha Dunn, "Proposition 2½: It's Right—It's Wrong—It's Not the Real Issue," *New England Journal of Human Services* 1, no. 4 (Fall 1981).

3 Many others share this expectation, already borne out by what was proposed and passed during the first year of the Reagan administration. See Sheldon S. Wolin, "Reagan Country," *New York Review of Books*, December 18, 1980; Jules M. Sugarman, "Human Services in the 1980's: A White Paper for Citizens and Government Officials," Washington, D.C. (Summer 1981); Allen Hunter, "In the Wings: New Right Organizations and Ideology," *Radical America* 15, nn. 1 and 2 (1981); and Frances Fox Piven and Richard A. Cloward, *The New Class War: Reagan's Attack on the Welfare State and Its Consequences* (New York: Pantheon, 1982).

4 See Laurence Lynn, *The State and Human Services: Organizational Change in a Political Context* (Cambridge, Mass.: MIT Press, 1980) and Bill Benton et al., *Social Services: Federal Legislation vs State Implementation* (Washington, D.C.: The Urban Institute, 1978) for examples of how other states have managed.

5 Many analysts have begun to consider how entrenched patterns change. See Herman Resnick and Rino J. Patti, eds., *Change from Within: Humanizing Social Welfare Organizations* (Philadelphia: Temple University Press, 1980); and George Brager and Steven Holloway, *Changing Human Service Organizations* (New York: Free Press, 1978). For classic treatments of bureaucratic inertia and change see Peter Blau and W. Richard Scott, *Formal Organizations* (San Francisco: Chandler, 1962), and Anthony Downs, *Inside Bureaucracy* (Boston: Little Brown, 1967).

2 The Circle Game

1 This is no longer the case, thanks to the action of legal advocates. Work-study funds are only counted against food stamp allowances, not against basic grants.

2   See Anthony Downs, *Inside Bureaucracy* (Boston: Little Brown, 1967); Peter Blau and W. Richard Scott, *Formal Organizations* (San Francisco: Chandler, 1962); and Amitai Etzioni, ed., *Complex Organizations: A Sociological Reader* (New York: Holt, Rinehart and Winston, 1961), for classic studies. See also Joel F. Handler, *The Deserving Poor: A Study of Welfare Administration* (Chicago: Markham Publishing Co., 1971); Michael Lipsky, *Street-Level Bureaucracy* (New York: Russell Sage Foundation, 1980), and Jeffrey M. Prottas, *People-Processing: The Street-Level Bureaucrat in Public Service Bureaucracies* (Lexington, Mass.: Lexington Books, 1979), for analysis of human service bureaucracies.

3   This approach is drawn, in a general way, from the arguments of André Gorz regarding "radical reformism" in *Socialism and Reform* (New York: Anchor Press, 1973).

4   Here the approach taken is in harmony with that taken by a broad spectrum of social welfare theorists. See the American writers John Romanyshyn, *Social Welfare: From Charity to Justice* (New York: Random House, 1971) and Harold Wilensky and Charles Lebeaux, *Industrial Society and Social Welfare* (New York: Free Press, 1965), as well as the British writer, Richard M. Titmuss, *Commitment to Welfare* (New York: Pantheon, 1968). These writers stress the gradual increase in rights to welfare. See also Ian Gough, *The Political Economy of the Welfare State* (London: Macmillan, 1979), and Colin Pritchard and Richard Taylor, *Social Work: Reform or Revolution?* (London: Routledge and Kegan Paul, 1978), who emphasize the "rights" gained through class struggle.

5   There is not much analytical history of conservative debate. However, some sense of the ongoing problems can be found in Theodor Allison, *Toward a Planned Society* (New York: Oxford University Press, 1975), James T. Patterson, *America's Struggle Against Poverty 1900–1980* (Cambridge, Mass.: Harvard University Press, 1981) and Gilbert Steiner, *Social Insecurity: The Politics of Welfare* (Chicago: Rand McNally, 1966).

6   Here Alfred J. Kahn is most important for arguing that social services are "social utilities." See his *Social Policy and Social Services* (New York: Knopf, 1973).

7   The most vocal perpetrators of this approach are Martin Anderson, *Welfare* (Stanford, Calif.: Hoover Institute, 1978), and writers published by the Washington-based conservative think tank, The Heritage Foundation, such as Charles D. Hobbs, *The Welfare Industry* (1978), and Onalee McGraw, *The Family, Feminism, and the Therapeutic State* (1980). But recent writings of such people as Christopher Lasch, *Haven in a Heartless World: The Family Besieged* (New York: Basic Books, 1979), and the contributors to *The Public Interest* help develop such notions also.

8   For a clear, short explanation of this premise, see Robert Morris, "Welfare Reform 1973: The Social Services Dimension" in *Science* 181 (August 1973).

9   William Ryan, *Blaming the Victim* (New York: Pantheon Books, 1971).

10   See *Public Welfare* 38, no. 1 (Winter 1980).

11   See Lipsky, *Street-Level Bureaucracy*, and Prottas, *People-Processing*, as well as David Street et al., *The Welfare Industry: Functionaries and Recipients in Public Aid* (Beverly Hills, Calif.: Sage Publications, 1979); Michael Greenblatt and Steve Richmond, *Public Welfare: Notes from Underground* (Cambridge, Mass.: Schenkman Publisher, 1979); and Robert Pruger, "The Good Bureaucrat," *Social Work* 18 (July 1973).

12 The information used here and later on current programs is very general and is derived from various sources. Most suggestive was the Massachusetts Taxpayers Foundation yearly report, "Budget Trends 1973–1982" (Boston: Massachusetts Taxpayers Foundation, 1981). Also helpful were the Department of Public Welfare's *Annual Reports* for 1980 and 1979 (Boston: Commonwealth of Massachusetts, 1980, 1981). For general information on clients served and number of employees I used "A Plan to Reorganize Human Services for the 1980's" published by the Massachusetts Executive Office of Human Services (1981). For Department of Mental Health figures I relied upon the report of The Blue Ribbon Commission on the Future of Public Inpatient Mental Health Services in Massachusetts, *Mental Health Crossroads*, S. Stephen Rosenfeld, Chairperson (Boston, May 1981). Also helpful for information on social services was the "Title XX Comprehensive Annual Service Plan for FY 81," put out by the Department of Social Services (1980).

It seems important to note here the difficulty in finding clear, noncontradictory information about state spending. Many reports use different formats and are especially confusing in regard to federal/state expenditure patterns. Here I have used general figures that seemed to be confirmed by more than one source. For my estimate of 750,000 clients, I took the Executive Office of Human Services' figure that 590,000 people received Medicaid as a base and compared it to their total of 1.7 million counted by all agencies. All AFDC and SSI are covered by Medicaid, so they did not need to be added, unlike the 22,000 GR recipients who receive another form of medical assistance. I considered that many of the 30,000 elderly served by DEA would not be eligible for Medicaid, as would not many of the 8,000 non-AFDC day care recipients, mentioned in the Title XX plan, or some of the 275,000 people receiving mental health services outside of institutions. I looked at the numbers receiving other services and decided that 750,000 seemed like a safe, conservative estimate, given there was no way to tell for sure how many discrete individuals received services. I would very much welcome hard, contradictory evidence from any source, even though Secretary Charles Mahoney's reorganization plan itself acknowledged that, "because of the lack of tracking systems and likely double counting of clients who bounce from agency to agency seeking services, it is not possible to obtain an accurate count of clients" (Massachusetts Executive Office of Human Services, *A Plan to Reorganize Massachusetts Human Services for the 1980's* [May 1980], p. 34).

Also, the 1980 census estimated that 10.4% of the people in Massachusetts are poor. For discussion of how difficult it is to define the number of poor people see Samuel Beer and Richard Barringer, eds., *The State and the Poor* (Cambridge, Mass.: Winthrop Publishers, 1970). This work also served as my source for the 1966 poverty figure.

One final source for understanding state programs, although not for budget figures, is the amazingly clear *Income Maximization Manual: For the Poor, the Aging and Those Getting Poorer in Massachusetts*, published by the Community Law Advocates Law Office, Greater Boston Legal Services and the Massachusetts Law Reform Institute (July 1980).

13 What it means to rise above poverty level is in dispute. Some, such as Martin Anderson, *Welfare*, argue that direct monetary and in-kind services (Medicaid, food stamps, social services) have pulled people out of poverty. Others, most recently the National Advisory Council on Economic Oppor-

tunity, argue that both relative and absolute poverty remain serious problems. See their *Critical Choices for the 80's* (Washington: U.S. Government Printing Office, 1980). Also see Beer and Barringer, *The State and the Poor.*

14   See *Is There Life after 2½* by the Policy Training Center, 10 West Street, Boston and Martha Dunn, "Proposition 2½: It's Right—It's Wrong—It's Not the Real Issue," *New England Journal of Human Services* 1, no. 4 (Fall 1981).

15   For the best exposition of this approach, see Charles F. Mahoney, executive secretary of Human Services, "Massachusetts: The Welfare State of America" distributed to the legislature in the spring of 1981 and "Preliminary Work and Welfare Proposal" by John M. Schlegell, October 14, 1981.

16   See the Blue Ribbon report, *Mental Health Crossroads.*

3 Up and Down and Around

1   The most important source for an overview of the Sargent administration is Margaret Weinberg, *Managing the State* (Cambridge, Mass.: MIT Press, 1977). Another important source is Martha Derthick, *The Influence of Federal Grants: Public Assistance in Massachusetts* (Cambridge, Mass.: Harvard University Press, 1970). For general analyses of Massachusetts politics, see also Edgar Litt, *The Political Culture of Massachusetts* (Cambridge, Mass.: MIT Press, 1965); and Murray B. Levin, *The Compleat Politician: Political Strategy in Massachusetts* (Indianapolis, Ind.: Bobbs Merrill, 1962).

2   See the National Study Services, *Meeting the Problems of People in Massachusetts: A Study of the Massachusetts Public Welfare System,* sponsored by Massachusetts Committee on Children and Youth and United Community Services of Metropolitan Boston (Boston: December 1965). The following discussion of how welfare worked in 1966 is taken largely from this report and from Weinberg, *Managing the State,* and Derthick, *The Influence of Federal Grants.*

3   Useful sources on information here are Weinberg, *Managing the State,* Denise Humm Delgado's "Community Living for Mentally Retarded Persons: Community Residences for Adults in Massachusetts" (Ph.D. diss., Brandeis University, 1977); the Blue Ribbon report, *Mental Health Crossroads,* S. Stephen Rosenfeld, Chairperson (Boston, May 1981); and Mental Hospital Planning Project, *Community Mental Health and the Mental Hospital* (Boston: United Community Planning Corporation, November 1973). Statistics are taken from Massachusetts Taxpayers Foundation, *State Budget Trends 1965–1973* (Boston, 1972).

4   For recent studies of the roots and implications of deinstitutionalization see Andrew Scull, *Decarceration: Community Treatment and the Deviant* (Englewood Cliffs, N.J.: Prentice Hall, 1977) and Steven P. Segal and Uri Aviram, *The Mentally Ill in Community-Based Sheltered Care* (New York: John Wiley and Sons, 1978).

5   See Weinberg, *Managing the State,* and Humm Delgado, "Community Living for Mentally Retarded Persons," for why it took so long for deinstitutionalization to occur.

6   National Study Service, *Meeting the Problems of People,* pp. 1–2.

7   See Frances Fox Piven and Richard A. Cloward, *Regulating the Poor: The Functions of Public Welfare* (New York: Pantheon, 1971). Their later work, *Poor People's Movements: Why They Succeed, How They Fail* (New York: Pantheon, 1977) offers in-depth analysis of the welfare rights movement and

its effects on policy changes in the 1960s. See also Sar Levitan and Robert Taggart, *The Promise of Greatness* (Cambridge, Mass.: Harvard University Press, 1976) for a different view of how services changed in the 1960s.

8   See Weinberg, *Managing the State,* and Derthick, *The Influence of Federal Grants.*

9   For a review of the arguments about why welfare rolls increased see Piven and Cloward, *Regulating the Poor;* James T. Patterson, *America's Struggle Against Poverty 1900–1980* (Cambridge, Mass.: Harvard University Press, 1981); and Kirsten A. Gornjberg, *Mass Society and the Extension of Welfare 1960–1970* (Chicago: University of Chicago Press, 1977).

10   See Piven and Cloward, *Poor People's Movements,* and Lawrence N. Bailis, *Bread or Justice: Grassroots Organizing in the Welfare Rights Movement* (Lexington, Mass.: Lexington Books, 1974).

11   Weinberg, *Managing the State,* pp. 152–53. Also see two Massachusetts Taxpayers Foundation publications, *Understanding Welfare: 1972* (Boston, 1972), and *Understanding Welfare: 1976* (Boston, December 1976).

12   See Harvard University's Center for Criminal Justice's five volume series on Youth Correctional Reform, especially Lloyd Ohlin, Robert Coates and Alden Miller, *Reforming Juvenile Corrections: The Massachusetts Experience* (Cambridge, Mass.: Ballinger, 1977), as well as Yitzhak Bakal, ed., *Closing Correctional Institutions: New Strategies for Youth Services* (Lexington, Mass.: Lexington Books, 1978) and also his work with Howard Polsky, *Reforming Corrections Institutions for Juvenile Offenders* (Lexington, Mass.: Lexington Books, 1979). See also the 1966 HEW *Study of the Division of Youth Services and the Youth Services Board of Massachusetts,* Washington, D.C., which led to the reorganization of youth services after its discovery by the *Boston Globe* in 1967.

13   This analysis is taken from an unpublished report on the secretariat prepared for the Area Strategy Office entitled "The Umbrella Human Service Agency" by Daniella Rath (1978). See also, "A Plan to Reorganize Massachusetts Human Services for the 1980s," published by the Massachusetts Executive Office of Human Services (May 1980).

14   To gain a sense of the complexity of welfare fraud, see Joel F. Handler, *The Deserving Poor: A Study of Welfare Administration* (Chicago: Markham Publishing Co., 1971) and his *Reforming the Poor* (New York: Basic Books, 1972); as well as Joe R. Feagin, *Subordinating the Poor: Welfare and American Beliefs* (Englewood Cliffs, N.J.: Prentice Hall, 1975) and Naomi Gottlieb, *The Welfare Bind* (New York: Columbia University Press, 1974).

15   See Michael Lipsky, *Street-Level Bureaucracy* (New York: Russell Sage Foundation, 1980); Jeffrey M. Prottas, *People-Processing: The Street Level Bureaucrat in Public Service Bureaucracies* (Lexington, Mass.: Lexington Books, 1979); Willard C. Richan and Allan R. Mendelsohn, *Social Work: The Unloved Profession* (New York: Franklin Watts, 1973) and Michael Greenblatt and Steve Richmond, *Public Welfare: Notes from Underground* (Cambridge, Mass.: Schenkman Publishing Co., 1979) for powerful studies of how service workers are trapped.

16   See Winifred Bell, "Too Few Services to Separate," in *Social Work* 18, no. 2 (March 1973). Also see Massachusetts Department of Public Welfare's "Plan for Separation of Services" (November 1972).

17   CHINS, however, did not become a full-scale program until 1978. Before then it only meant a new group of children for whom the department was

somehow responsible. For sources on efforts to decriminalize status offenders see *Report of the White House Conference on Youth* (Washington, D.C.: U.S. Government Printing Office, 1971); *Youth: Transition to Adulthood*, Report of the Panel on Youth of the President's Science Advisory Committee (Chicago: University of Chicago Press, 1974); and Pat Wald, "Making Sense out of the Rights of Youth," *Child Welfare* 145 (June 1976).

18 Massachusetts Taskforce on Children Out of School, *Suffer the Children* (Boston: Massachusetts Advocacy Center, 1972).

19 See Weinberg, *Managing the State*, and W. Robert Curtis "From State Hospital to Integrated Human Services: Managing the Transition," *Health Care Management Review* 4, no. 12 (1976).

20 See all volumes of the Harvard Center for Criminal Justice study, n. 12 above.

21 I am indebted to Sandra Frawley, "Bureaucratic Competition and Policy Implementation" (Ph.D. diss., Brandeis University, 1977) for this analysis.

22 See Frawley, "Bureaucratic Competition and Policy Implementation," pp. 164–166.

23 See Rath, "The Umbrella Service Agency."

24 See the DPW studies, "Sample of General Relief 'Employable' Recipients" (August 1975), and "Termination of General Relief Cash and Medical Assistance to Employable Individuals: A Four Month Follow-Up Study" (May 1976), both by Gail Shields. Also see Mass. Taxpayers Foundation, *Understanding Welfare: 1976*.

25 Greenblatt and Richmond, *Public Welfare*, p. 12. See also unpublished study done for SEIU 509 by the Massachusetts Labor Research Group, "An Analysis of Proposed Productivity Methods and Standards for Assistance Payments and Medical Assistance Units of the Massachusetts Department of Public Welfare" (November 1979), as well as an unpublished paper by Andrew S. Natsios, "Jerry Stevens and the Department of Public Welfare" (n.d.). (Available from its author, who is a Massachusetts State Representative.)

26 I was involved in this effort to produce a workable system for Massachusetts social service workers. Alas, many of the problems I had studied regarding the uneasy relationships between universities and state agencies came to life in this attempt. See "Training for Social Services in Public Welfare Agencies and the Role of Institutions of Higher Education" by Charles I. Schottland, Principal Investigator, and Ilana Hirsch Lescohier and Ann Withorn, Associate Project Directors (unpublished report prepared under SRS Grant No. 84-P-9026711-01, February 1977).

27 Massachusetts General Laws, Article 522, July, 1978. I am indebted to Lennie Marcus of the Heller School, Brandeis University, for helping me better understand the forces that led to the creation of DSS. His insights will be published in his forthcoming dissertation at the Florence Heller School, Brandeis University.

28 See Children's Services Taskforce, *The Children's Puzzle*, Institute for Governmental Services, University of Massachusetts/Boston (1977), pp. 9–11. See also an earlier unpublished document from the Executive Office of Human Services, "Final Revision of the Taskforce Report of Children and Family Services Reorganization," 1976, which suggested similar options.

29 *Children's Puzzle*, pp. 11–12.

30 See Curtis, "From State Hospital to Integrated Human Services," and *Area Based Human Services* (Boston: SMRI Publications, 1979).

4   Special Effects

1   See June Axinn and Herman Levin, *Social Welfare: A History of the American Response to Need* (New York: Dodd, Mead, 1975); Robert Morris, *Social Policy in the American Welfare State* (New York: Harper and Row, 1979); as well as Laurence Lynn, *The State and Human Services* (Cambridge, Mass.: MIT Press, 1980); and Martha Derthick, *The Influence of Federal Grants* (Cambridge, Mass.: Harvard University Press, 1970).

2   See Robert D. Plotnick and Felicity Skidmore, *Progress Against Poverty: A Review of the 1964–1974 Decade* (New York: Academic Press, 1975); National Advisory Council on Economic Opportunity, *Critical Choices for the 80's* (Washington, D.C.: U.S. Government Printing Office, 1980); Martha Derthick, *Uncontrollable Spending for Social Service Grants* (Washington, D.C.: The Brookings Institution, 1975); and Derthick, *The Influence of Federal Grants;* Bill Benton et al., *Social Services: Federal Legislation vs State Implementation* (Washington, D.C.: The Urban Institute, 1978); and Robert Morris, Ilana Lescohier, and Ann Withorn, "Analysis of Federally Supported Social Services," prepared under HEW contract No. SA-7726-77 September 1977.

3   For the best summary of poverty programs, see Sar Levitan and Robert Taggart, *The Promise of Greatness* (Cambridge, Mass.: Harvard University Press, 1976).

4   See Andrew Scull, *Decarceration: Community Treatment and the Deviant* (Englewood Cliffs, N.J.: Prentice Hall, 1977); and Levitan and Taggart, *Promise of Greatness.*

5   My sense of how this operates comes from discussions with federal professionals over the years, especially in context of my research on Title XX services and training. See also Laurence Lynn, *The State and Human Services* (Cambridge, Mass.: MIT Press, 1980).

6   One of the major frustrations of this study was the difficulty in tracking the total amounts of federal moneys that come into the state. Although the major reimbursable programs (Medicaid, AFDC, Title XX) yield reliable figures, I found that the total amount that comes in as direct grants to public or private agencies was extremely difficult to determine. The Massachusetts Foundation does a monumental job of tracking these numbers in their yearly "Budget Trends."

7   Again, see Morris, *Social Policy in the American Welfare State,* as well as Benton et al., *Social Services.* For general treatment of how American federalism affects the human services see Robert Morris, "The Human Service Function and Local Government," *Managing Human Services,* ed. Wayne Anderson et al. (Washington, D.C.: Institute for Training in Municipal Administration. 1977).

8   E. Digby Baltzell, *Puritan Boston and Quaker Philadelphia* (New York: The Free Press, 1979). Also see Derthick, *The Influence of Federal Grants.*

9   Michael Lipsky, in *Street-Level Bureaucracy* (New York: Russell Sage Foundation, 1980), fully documents how this occurs.

10   See Joel Handler, *Protecting the Social Service Client: Legal and Constitutional Limits of Official Discretion* (New York: Academic Press, 1979), for a guide to legal advocacy as well as the publications of the Center on Welfare Policy and Law, 95 Madison Avenue, New York, New York 10016.

11   Conversations with public relations staff at Boston-area television stations suggested that in 1966 the three network stations only provided limited

daily local news coverage. Today all have large news departments developing local stories as well as locally produced discussion/talk shows, which
often cover human service issues.

12   For summaries of the increase in public spending on private agencies see
Ilana Hirsch Lescohier, "Identifying Trends in Social Service Provisions under the Public Assistance Titles and Title XX of the Social Security Act"
(Ph.D. diss., Brandeis University, 1979); Massachusetts Taxpayers Founda-
tions, Inc., *Purchase of Service: Can State Government Gain Control?* (1980)
and Arnold Gurin and Barry Friedman, Project Directors, "Contracting for
Services as a Mechanism for the Delivery of Human Services: A Study of
Contracting Practices in Three Human Services Agencies in Massachusetts,"
unpublished report, OHDS Grant No. 18P-0017011-01 (1980). All three studies contain helpful bibliographies.

13   I owe my understanding of this series of events to Jack Walsh, a political
consultant who was actively involved in the process.

5   The Department of Public Welfare
as Designated Patient

1   Most of these costs were funded under Title IVB of the Social Security Act
—the Child Welfare provisions. Some were also funded as social service
costs under the AFDC provision of that same act, Title IVA.

2   Another way to accomplish this (suggested by Betty Reid Mandell) would
be to see the distribution of income supports as a simple clerking function,
similar to the disbursement of Social Security checks. Then eligibility could
be determined sporadically with random reviews for accuracy, similar to
IRS. My sense is that such an approach is an ideal goal but highly unlikely
until some basic economic structures change in this society. What I propose is a more interim shift in approach which might lead to the level
of consciousness necessary for such a desired change. See Betty Reid Mandell, "Whose Welfare? An Introduction" in *Welfare in America: Controlling
the Dangerous Classes,* ed. Betty R. Mandell (Englewood Cliffs, N.J.: Prentice Hall, 1975).

6   Power and Protection

1   There was also a new field of community mental health emerging during
this time which gave planners and workers the theoretical support for
changes. See Joint Commission on Mental Illness and Health, *Action for
Mental Health* (New York: Basic Books, 1961); G. Caplan, *Support Systems
and Community Mental Health* (New York: Behavioral Publications, 1978);
and B.L. Bloom, *Community Mental Health* (Monterey, Calif.: Brooks-Cole
Publishing, 1977).

2   See unpublished Ford Foundation study by Robert Morris, Ilana Lescohier
and Ann Withorn, "Social Service Delivery Systems: Attempts to Alter
Local Patterns 1970–1974" (Waltham, Mass.: Brandeis University, 1975).
Statistics on mental-health expenditures taken from the 1980 *Annual Report,* Massachusetts Department of Public Welfare, and the 1980 "Comprehensive Social Services Plan," published by DSS.

3   One version of this analysis was given as a talk by Scott Bass, "Key Players,

Power and Decision Making" at the Minority Mental Health Conference (Boston, 1981).

4   See Karl Deutsch, *The Nerves of Government* (New York: Free Press, 1963), as well as more recent essays in the highly suggestive collection, Herman Resnick and Rino J. Patti, eds., *Changes from Within: Humanizing Social Welfare Organizations* (Philadelphia: Temple University Press, 1980).

7   The Ties That Bind

1   See Margaret Weinberg, *Managing the State* (Cambridge, Mass.: MIT Press, 1977).

2   See Laurence Lynn, *Managing the Public Business* (New York: Basic Books, 1981); Wayne F. Anderson et al., eds., *Managing Human Services* (Washington, D.C.: International City Management Association, 1977); and Richard Steiner, *Managing the Human Service Organizations* (Beverly Hills, Calif.: Sage Publications, 1977).

3   Of course, such problems are not new to bureaucracies. See Fred A. Kramer, ed., *Perspectives in Public Bureaucracy*, 3d ed. (Cambridge, Mass.: Winthrop Publishers, 1981); Peter Blau and W. Richard Scott, *Formal Organizations* (San Francisco: Chandler, 1962); and Anthony Downs, *Inside Bureaucracy* (Boston: Little Brown, 1967); as well as the more hopeful recent works by Herman Resnick and Rino J. Patti, eds., *Change from Within: Humanizing Social Welfare Organizations* (Philadelphia: Temple University Press, 1980) and George Brager and Steven Holloway, *Changing Human Service Organizations* (New York: Free Press, 1978).

4   See Andrew Scull, *Decarceration* (Englewood Cliffs, N.J.: Prentice Hall, 1978) and such critiques as "From Hospitals to Jails: The Fate of California's Deinstitutionalized Mentally Ill," *American Journal of Orthopsychiatry* 50, no. 1 (1980).

5   The issue of professionalism has long plagued the social work and human service world. See such classics as Abraham Flexner, "Is Social Work a Profession?," *Proceedings of the National Conference of Charities and Corrections* (Chicago: The Hilderman Company, 1915); and Roy Lubove, *The Professional Altruist: The Emergence of Social Work as a Profession* (Cambridge, Mass.: Harvard University Press, 1965); as well as books such as Willard Richan and Allan R. Mendelsohn, *Social Work: The Unloved Profession* (New York: Franklin Watts, 1973); Nina Toren, *Social Work: The Case of a Semi-Profession* (Beverly Hills, Calif.: Sage Publications, 1972); and Robert Cohen, *New Careers Grows Older: A Perspective on the Paraprofessional Experience 1965–1975* (Baltimore: Johns Hopkins University Press, 1977).

6   This should not be too surprising, given the findings of such writers as Joel Handler in *Reforming the Poor* (New York: Basic Books, 1972); Richard M. Elman in *The Poorhouse State* (New York: Dell, 1968); Rosalie Boehme, "Social Services: Recipients Want But Don't Get," *Public Welfare* 30, no. 1 (Winter 1972); and Lewis Coser "What do the Poor Need? (Money)," in *The Sociology of American Poverty*, ed. Joan Huber and H. Paul Chalfant (Cambridge, Mass.: Shenkman Publishing Company, 1974).

7   These issues reappear throughout the history of social welfare literature. A good place to see the consistent patterns is in a review of the annual *Proceedings* of the National Conference on Social Welfare, which have been

published for over one hundred and twenty-five years by Columbia University Press.

8   The best clear argument of this position is Martin Anderson, *Welfare* (Stanford, Calif.: Hoover Institute, 1978).

9   See Ilana Hirsch Lescohier, "Identifying Trends in Social Service Provisions under the Public Assistance Titles and Title XX of the Social Security Act" (Ph.D. diss., Brandeis University, 1979); Laurence Lynn, *The State and Human Services: Organizational Change in a Political Context* (Cambridge, Mass.: MIT Press, 1980); and Bill Benton et al., *Social Services: Federal Legislation vs State Implementation* (Washington, D.C.: The Urban Institute, 1978).

10   See Frances Fox Piven and Richard A. Cloward, *Regulating the Poor* (New York: Pantheon, 1971) and *The New Class War* (New York: Pantheon, 1982); as well as Ian Gough, *The Political Economy of the Welfare State* (London: Macmillan, 1979); and James O'Connor, *The Fiscal Crisis of the State* (New York: St. Martins Press, 1973).

11   Figures taken from *Encyclopedia of Social Work* (New York: NASW, 1976). See Sar Levitan and Robert Taggart, *The Promise of Greatness* (Cambridge, Mass.: Harvard University Press, 1976). Also, President Reagan is considering a federal takeover of Medicaid, in exchange for full state funding of welfare and food stamps. Is this perhaps another indication that the doctors, not the poor people, will be protected in the social "safety net"?

12   See *Social Security in America's Future: Final Report of the National Commission on Social Security* (Washington, D.C.: National Commission on Social Security, March 1981); and the *Annual Report, 1980*, Massachusetts Department of Public Welfare, Boston, Massachusetts.

13   See Martha Derthick, *Uncontrollable Spending for Social Services Grants* (Washington, D.C.: Brookings Institution, 1975); and Ilana Lescohier, *Identifying Trends*.

14   See The Research Group, Inc., *Integration of Human Services in HEW*, vol. 1 (Washington, D.C., 1972); Gerald Horton et al., *Illustrating Services Integration from Categorical Bases*, Project Share Monograph no. 3 (November 1976, Washington, D.C.); Sidney Gartner, *Roles for General Purpose Governments in Services Integration*, Project Share Monograph no. 2 (Washington, D.C.: HEW, 1976). These and other efforts are criticized in Robert Morris and Ilana Hirsch Lescohier, "Services Integration: Real vs Illusory Solutions to Welfare Dilemmas" (Paper given at a conference on "Issues in Service Delivery in Human Service Organizations," June 1977).

15   I was, I must confess, one of those eager graduate-student researchers.

16   See Joe R. Feagin, *Subordinating the Poor: Welfare and American Beliefs* (Englewood Cliffs, N.J.: Prentice Hall, 1975); Herbert J. Gans, "The Positive Functions of Poverty," *American Journal of Sociology* 78 (September 1972); Paul T. Therkildsen, *Public Assistance and American Values* (Albuquerque: University of New Mexico Press, 1964); and Lester M. Salamon, ed., *Welfare: The Elusive Consensus* (New York: Praeger Special Studies, 1978).

17   Michael Lipsky, *Street-Level Bureaucracy* (New York: Russell Sage Foundation, 1980).

8   Will the Circle Be Unbroken?

1   I owe my understanding of these issues in large part to conversations with Allen Hunter regarding his forthcoming Brandeis University dissertation on

the New Right, as well as to his article, "In the Wings: New Right Organizations and Ideology," *Radical America* 15, nos. 1 and 2 (1981). Also John Brouder, who led a coalition to fight Proposition 2½, has convinced me that our local Citizens for Limited Taxation group shares many of the hard-core assumptions.

2 Here the source is, of course, George Gilder, *Wealth and Poverty* (New York: Basic Books, 1981), as well as Martin Anderson, *Welfare* (Stanford, Calif.: Hoover Institute, 1978).

3 Again, see Gilder, *Wealth and Poverty*, and Onalee McGraw, *The Family, Feminism, and the Therapeutic State* (Washington, D.C.: Heritage Foundation, 1980).

4 Here the best sources are again Gilder, *Wealth and Poverty*, but also the entire reading list of the Heritage Foundation, 513 C Street, N.E., Washington, D.C. 20002. Allen Hunter, again, has been central to my understanding of the divisions within conservative thought.

5 A helpful discussion of this disjuncture between popular support and New Right ideology is to be found in Frances Fox Piven and Richard A. Cloward, *The New Class War: Reagan's Attack on the Welfare State and Its Consequences* (New York: Pantheon, 1982).

6 I have discussed this group more fully elsewhere. See "Beyond Realism: Fighting for Human Services in the 1980's," *Catalyst: A Socialist Journal of the Social Services* 3 (Fall 1982).

7 The clearest statement of this position in Massachusetts was made by Charles Francis Mahoney, first secretary of Human Services under Governor King, in his paper "Massachusetts: The Welfare State of America," which was circulated to legislators and the general public in the summer of 1981.

8 See the Policy Training Center for its materials and brochures, 10 West Street, Boston, Massachusetts.

9 See Piven and Cloward, *The New Class War*, for a discussion of how this works, as well as Elizabeth Wilson, *Women and the Welfare State* (Tavistock: Tavistock Publishers, 1977).

10 For the best discussions of this ambivalence see Ian Gough, *The Political Economy of the Welfare State* (London: Macmillan, 1979); Paul Corrigan and Peter Leonard, *Social Work Practice under Capitalism* (London: Macmillan, 1978); and Jeffry Galper, *Radical Social Work* (Englewood Cliffs, N.J.: Prentice Hall, 1980).

11 A new British journal, *Critical Social Policy*, distributed by Pluto Press, is attempting to directly confront such issues in a serious, complex way.

12 This image was suggested by an anonymous review of this manuscript and reinforced by a column by Ellen Goodman in the January 1982, *Boston Globe*.

13 See Bob Deacon, "Social Administration, Social Policy and Socialism" in *Critical Social Policy* 1, no. 1 (Fall 1981), for a critical discussion of this vision. See also my article "The Limits and Potential of Self Help" in *Radical America* 14, no. 3 (May/June 1980).

14 I am grateful to Mary Jo Hetzel for sharing the early results of a dissertation for the University of Massachusetts, Political Science Department, which show that the problem of hierarchy and lack of control are central issues for human service workers.

15 A "Plan to Reorganize Human Services for the 1980's" was submitted by the out-going secretary of Human Services, Charles F. Mahoney in July 1981.

Index